Continuous Process Improvement

Simplifying Work Flow Systems

GEORGE D. ROBSON

THE FREE PRESS
A Division of Macmillan, Inc.
NEW YORK

Maxwell Macmillan Canada
TORONTO

Maxwell Macmillan International
NEW YORK   OXFORD   SINGAPORE   SYDNEY

The Free Press
A Division of Macmillan, Inc.
866 Third Avenue, New York, N.Y. 10022

Maxwell Macmillan Canada, Inc.
1200 Eglinton Avenue East
Suite 200
Don Mills, Ontario M3C 3N1

Macmillan, Inc. is part of the Maxwell Communication Group of Companies.

Printed in the United States of America

printing number
1 2 3 4 5 6 7 8 9 10

Library of Congress Cataloging-in-Publication Data

Robson, George D.
    Continuous process improvement / George D. Robson.
      p.   cm.
    ISBN 0–02–926645–9
    1. Production management.   2. Process control.   3. Production engineering.   I. Title.
    TS155.R596   1991
    658.5—dc20   91–9808
                                                            CIP

*To Donna Kay, my mom, and the memory
of my dad*

Contents

Preface   **vii**
Acknowledgments   **x**

1 **Why Bother?**   **1**

What is CPI?   *4*
What can CPI do for us?   *7*
Business benefits   *9*
How does CPI work?   *14*
Tools and techniques   *26*
Brainstorming   *29*
Storyboarding   *30*
Why does CPI work?   *35*
What makes CPI continuous?   *41*
Real time application assignment   *57*

2 **Getting Started**   **59**

How do you know where to look?   *59*
Process flow concept   *60*
Process flow diagraming (PFD)   *67*
What do we look for?   *73*
Real time application assignment   *76*

3 **What's Critical?**   **79**

Deciding what to do first   *79*
Stating the problem   *86*
Analyzing the problem   *88*
Real time application assignment   *102*

4 **Listening to Your Process**   **105**

Process performance   *106*
Process capability   *110*
Specifications vs. process capability   *114*
Variability   *118*
Variability and control   *120*
Control charts   *126*
Control limits   *129*
Practical use of control charts   *131*
Real time application assignment   *149*

5 **The Next Step**   **151**

A few reminders   *152*
Implementing corrective action   *153*
Making a presentation   *166*
Project requirements   *170*
Team meetings   *172*
The role of management   *175*
Commitment   *177*

Index   **179**

Preface

FRESH OUT OF COLLEGE, I was ready to meet the challenges the world had to offer. I had learned all there was to learn and I was prepared to make some significant changes. However, I wasn't exactly sure how to begin my quest. I soon discovered that was the way most other newly graduated engineers felt, also. However, I came in contact with a breed of engineer referred to as "Co-op's." These people seemed to look at the world through different-colored glasses. They seemed to adapt more quickly, and it appeared they had gained more from their educational experience than those without the co-op experience. As I moved from business to business in the early stages of my career, I noted the difference was not peculiar to one company. Rather, there appeared to be a prevalent distinction between the two groups, i.e. those who experienced applied learning in contrast to those who didn't.

As I moved into management, I noted that those people who had the co-op experience and those with hands-on practical application of what they learned were much more effective employees. And they appeared to have a greater appreciation of the bigger business picture than those without a similar experience.

My role as a corporate consultant provided additional valuable observations. I noted that even though people attended traditional classroom training and education and emerged with a firm grasp of new or newly reinforced concepts, practical application sometimes seemed foreign and was viewed as "something extra" to contend with. They failed to make the tie between the educational experience and accomplishment of daily work.

As I worked with people from various educational levels and intermixed groups of managers and individual contributors, another noteworthy characteristic emerged. If a group of people experienced a common learning event in a friendly, trusting, supportive environment, the event tended to reinforce their teamwork. If this team was then shown how to apply the learning experience to help better perform their daily work, they readily adapted the new skills or learning experience to the workplace.

Another observation which appeared to cover the full spectrum of people and positions was that most people liked to be shown how to apply what they learned for their personal benefit. Once shown, they readily accepted assistance in adapting it to areas where it could most benefit their team.

One final important observation. As I read textbooks and business books, I noted there was almost always something missing, i.e., practical, reinforced application of newly learned concepts. Or, they were filled with wonderful stories of success, and application was left as "an exercise for the student." I was usually left impressed and exhilarated but with a big "so what?". There was always the question of "How do I do it?" left lingering after the book was closed.

It was the accumulation of these experiences and observations tied to the lingering question "How do I do it?" that ultimately compelled me to write this book. The methodology revealed as you progress from chapter to chapter will help you personally answer the lingering question and will lead you from just talking about what to do to translating some well established and widely known tools and techniques into practical application. Beware, CPI is not a panacea. It doesn't happen miraculously or instantaneously. Implementation and success requires a lot of hard work and is founded in commitment and "ownership" by each individual involved. As you progress through the book, consider the roles you play and investment you must make to ensure success. If you choose to make the investment, it can repay handsomely.

When I graduated from Penn State, I received a very special and inspirational bit of advice from my parents. I find myself revisiting the eloquent and wise philosophy from time to time and feel it appropriate to share it with you in the opening pages of this book. My Dad, the late William T. Robson, Jr., was a lover of poetry, and he composed a personal message for the occasion. It represents the simple but practical philosophy used throughout CPI.

If you can't be a pine on the top of the hill,
Be a scrub in the valley—but be
The best little scrub by the side of the rill,
Be a bush if you can't be a tree.

If you can't be a highway, just be a trail.
If you can't be the sun be a star;
It isn't the size, that you win or fail!!!
Be the best of whatever you are.

Acknowledgments

THIS BOOK is a reality only through the support and encouragement of many. The risk of recognizing specific contributions can lead to possible oversights. Therefore, to all my contributing colleagues who go unnamed but have contributed to this work, I extend my sincere appreciation.

My initial acknowledgments are to Steve Hegyi, with whom the initial thoughts and ideas were generated and developed; and to Dr. R. M. Anderson and Dick Smith, for their support and confidence. Specific recognition goes to Paula Wright for her invaluable implementation support and to Bob Piselli for his creative talents in graphic representations.

A note of thanks goes to Dick Hilbert for recognizing the broad applied value of CPI and for his personal support in critique, development, and publication of the manuscript. Special recognition and personal thanks go to Dr. J. P. Baughman for his support, without which this book would not exist. To Norah Moneypenny goes a well deserved thank you and lifelong indebtedness for her patience and skillful preparation of the manuscript.

In addition, I owe a great deal to Jack Sahl for his legal guidance, encouragement, and personal attention. I also express my gratitude to all those people who saw the value of the process and were courageous enough to put it into daily business practice. To Frank Weimann, Bob Wallace, and the support staff at The Free Press, I extend my appreciation for expert guidance.

To Alaina, Dan, and Julie, my thanks for understanding the time this took away from our family relationship. The results I share with each of you.

Last but not least, I want to thank my wife, Donna Kay, for her patience, her never-ending faith in me, and the strength and encouragement she provided when I needed them most.

1

Why Bother?

DURING THE THIRD QUARTER OF 1989, the service arm of a major corporation (for convenience and anonymity we'll refer to it as SERVCO) projected that they would exceed their revenue target for the year and began to address their goals for 1990. The challenge was to continue to increase revenue, hold current manpower levels relatively constant, reduce inventory, "significantly" improve cycle time across the entire operation, reduce the supplier base, keep current customers happy, and expand the number of customers for whom they were performing repairs and product overhauls. Sound familiar?

Faced with the formidable task of trying to achieve these goals, the staff began looking for a starting point. The one thing that kept appearing as their customers' highest priority was "the time to repair hardware." The perception was that it always took too long. Factoring this in with corporate expectations, they chose to approach their task in a nontraditional way by using continuous process improvement (CPI) methodology, tools, and techniques. Rather than trying to attack all things in their previous reactive, firefighting manner, they decided to focus on reduction of repair cycle time and tie all other efforts to it.

The change began by narrowing their purview to the "critical few" processes considered essential to attaining business plans and goals which included reduction of repair cycle time. The initial focus was narrowed to five processes for which natural teams were selected for CPI training.

Let's digress briefly from SERVCO's problems to determine what this thing called CPI really is. The objectives here are (1) to introduce you to the general concept of continuous process improvement and (2) to help you develop a working definition of CPI from a personal perspective and from the viewpoint of your "natural work team." If you're wondering what is meant by the term "natural work team," it's all the people who work together daily and "own" a particular process. We'll get into the process ownership concept in the section "Why does CPI work?"

CPI is fundamentally a toolbox of skills and techniques applied with a simple methodology to stimulate continuous improvement and control of processes. The processes are in turn used to satisfy customer needs and expectations, both internal and external to a business.

Take a moment to define, in your own words, the meaning of the word "process." If you are working with a team, and you should be to get the maximum benefit from this book, share your definition with all your team members. Then consider Webster's* definition:

> *Process:* A particular method of doing something, generally involving a number of steps or operations.

Compare your definition with Webster's and decide if you need to alter yours. Typically, people have found that the dictionary version reinforces what they initially recorded. Before sharing any further thoughts or definitions with your team, let's get back to the business scenario.

SERVCO opted to begin the process in a nontraditional manner with a heavy commitment to management training. They wanted to send the message through the organization, "We're serious about this."

The process began as a pilot in the fourth quarter of 1989. Doing the right thing at the right time was of supreme importance. By beginning training and implementation at a time when the traditional focus was primarily on meeting year-end shipments at all cost, the management team sent another clear message that things would be different. They were and still are.

As you might expect, along with the changes came some good

---

* As you progress through the book, you will find dictionary definitions which were obtained from the following two sources: *Webster's New World Dictionary of the American Language, Second College Edition* (William Collins and World Publishing Company, Inc., Cleveland, 1976) and *New American Webster Handy College Dictionary* (Signet, New York, 1981).

news and some bad. The good news was that repair cycle times had been reduced in more than ten major business processes. Improvements ranged from 24% to 60%, and all were accomplished by the natural teams, with the support and direct involvement of the management team. Some teams involved key suppliers in the process and none required or recommended capital expenditures. After one year of training and implementation, SERVCO had 28 active process improvement projects that applied CPI methodology on a daily basis with an average reduction of 47% in repair cycle time.

The bad (but not unexpected) news was that the real world still existed. Change from the previous modus operandi was going to take time, patience, and persistence. The modified processes and implementation of the methodology were healthy albeit fragile. A few skeptics were still not buying into the process, causing opposing challenges the management team would rather not have to cope with. However, the team persisted, the process worked, and the results were well worth the effort.

Business plans for the future took on a clear focus involving customer needs and supplier partnerships. The improvement purview was expanded to include processes related to inventory while maintaining customer satisfaction and further reducing cycle time. A clear message was sent that the business would continue to integrate CPI methodology into management and daily activities.

This business grew and flourished because the management team chose to do things differently. They continue to use the simple tools and techniques of CPI to ensure customer satisfaction and improve daily operating processes. The dramatic reductions in repair cycle time not only led to improved customer satisfaction, they also translated directly into improvement of the bottom line. What more could a business want than a growing clientele, a healthy balance sheet, and a successful launch into a rapidly changing and challenging decade?

The global business world of the 1990s represents an arena where complacent businesses, managers, and others who are not receptive to change will most likely perish. To survive, let alone flourish, businesses in the '90s must meet the ever increasing and more demanding challenges of:

- Dynamic customer expectations
- Expanding worldwide competition
- Strategically implementing state-of-the-art technology

A strong, healthy business today is the direct result of meeting the challenges of the past. However, to remain strong and productive and be the natural choice of the customers, some changes will most probably be required.

If you don't believe what you've read so far, or if you don't intend to open yourself to change to meet the challenges of the 1990s and the twenty-first century, don't bother reading any further. Why? Because you and the people around you will most probably be doing something else in the very near future. If you haven't figured out the answer to "Why bother?" it's because business as usual isn't good enough!

However, if you do believe what you've read so far, the information and methodology presented in the following pages can help you improve your business. As you proceed, remember that CPI is not a panacea, nor is it a solution looking for a problem to solve. Proof exists to illustrates that it is possible for any business to experience SERVCO's success. There is nothing magical about it. Simply apply the methodology presented in the following chapters. Be aware that it takes leadership, time, patience, and persistence to make it happen and last. It's entirely up to the business team members whether they choose to change or chance ending up a casualty of the 1990s. CPI can help make that change successful.

What Is CPI?

Ground Rules

Before getting started with the logic, skills, and techniques that make up CPI, let's establish some fundamental ground rules for creating the appropriate environment. They must be treated as canonical and adhered to at all times. It is essential that these ground rules be clearly articulated, understood, and abided by within each and every team and that they are fully supported at and by all levels of management. All successful CPI teams follow these basics. As you peruse and internalize them, you will begin to understand why they are emphasized.

1. *Be open.* Don't be afraid to share an idea. Remember, it's yours and it represents an expression of yourself. As you listen to other people's ideas, be open, supportive, or passive. Never attack! It kills ideas and erodes trust.

2. *Be supportive and noncritical.* When someone expresses an idea, be supportive and you'll be surprised how it is returned. Contribute in a noncritical manner. Remember, criticism kills ideas. Open support nurtures and encourages participation and builds trust.

3. *Be positive.* After listening to an idea or comment, respond positively. Try forcing yourself to say something like, "I like that idea because . . ." Remember, around every donut hole there is a donut.

4. *Be willing to share your thoughts and feelings.* Express your ideas no matter how insignificant or dumb you think they might be. When you share your thoughts and feelings you make yourself vulnerable. You will discover that when you are vulnerable, most people will want to help. Open sharing is a great team-building activity.

5. *No finger pointing.* Never be threatening. Remember to check your hand to see how many fingers are pointing back at yourself when you point at someone else.

6. K.I.S.S. (Keep it straightforward and simple). This is a cardinal rule of CPI. If you are tempted to try to make something complex, don't. If you are attempting to solve a complex problem or address a complex process, break it down to its simplest form, then proceed.

7. *Have fun.* When people have fun together, the stress level goes down, defenses go down, and creativity is enhanced. Never take yourself too seriously. I still hate to hear my wife tell me to "lighten up." But it always works. Learn to laugh at yourself or a bad situation. Remember, only you can control your attitude and outlook.

Defining CPI

Recalling the earlier exercise where you defined "process," now expand your definitions to include the terms *continuous* and *improvement.* Webster defines these terms as:

Continuous: Going on or extending without interruption or break, unbroken, connected.

Improvement: An increase in value or in excellence of quality or condition.

Using your definitions and the reinforcement of Webster, your team should develop and record a definition of continuous process improvement. When your discussion has achieved a consensus, make sure it is reinforced by Webster's terminology.

Since you have now decided on a definition of CPI, let's discuss what it is not.

CPI Is Not Just Another Program

A typical program has a beginning and an end. It exists for a finite period of time and is usually created to accomplish a single specific goal before being discarded. In contrast, CPI has a beginning, but it has no end until the process it is associated with is no longer a functioning part of the business and has been eliminated or replaced by another process of greater value. And this is only where the differences begin. Later when we address the topic "Why does CPI work?" you will have an opportunity to explore further the characteristics of programs and how they differ from CPI.

From this point forward you are instructed to strike the word "program" from your vocabulary when you speak of CPI. It will not be easy, but it will help you achieve the fundamental change required to make CPI the way you think and do your job. A question that always arises is, "How much time do you expect me to spend on this? I still have my job to do, you know." My response has always been met with inquisitive looks and silence from managers and individual contributors alike:

> I expect you to spend forty or more hours a week on the process because it must become the way you do your job. It can't be something extra to do. It must become the way you think and act every day. It must become such a part of what you do and how you do it that eventually you will be doing it without talking about it.

CPI is a proven prevention and improvement system built on four basic principles:

- Continuous improvement must be a way of life.
- Problems must be prevented rather than reacted to.
- Results must be measurable and directly related to business plans and goals.
- Team ownership of a process is essential.

The process helped several businesses identify and implement total savings in excess of $35 million from simple process improvements during the first two years of its use. By calculating the ratio of dollars spent on training and identified business savings, you arrive at an impressive 80 to 1 return on the training investment.

CPI consists of a logical set of simple and straightforward steps that are used by "natural work teams" to analyze and understand the processes they use in their work and to focus on the critical parts of those processes that require attention. Initially it provides a systematic way of eliminating the unnecessary, nonessential, non-value-adding parts of the process followed by continuous improvement of the simplified, streamlined process. It is a transportable process that is not only applicable to "manufacturing" type processes, but has proven applicable and powerful in a variety of business processes. You will see examples of various team activities in case studies and project summaries as you proceed through the text and begin to gain personal experience with the tools and techniques.

What Can CPI Do for Us?

Now that we've briefly explored what CPI is and how it involves the management team, let's look at the value it holds for the individual members of natural work teams. Basically, we want to answer that age-old question, "What's in it for me?" But in this case let's begin by asking the question from the team point of view: "What's in it for us?"

You don't need to be an international economist or CEO of a major corporation to understand that we are living and working in a complex world. We have seen technology shrink the world and launch us into a global economy that has forced us to think and act in a strategically different way. We find ourselves faced with more and larger problems while still dealing with the nitty-gritty things we must do just to survive. Many businesses have proven that by adopting CPI as a business strategy, they have been effective in meeting the challenges of worldwide competition by:

- Overcoming complacency
- Attacking the things they've learned to live with
- Getting rid of non-value-added work
- Preventing problems rather than reacting to them
- Continuously improving all business processes

From the individual team's perspective it does much more by simply:

- Focusing attention on detail
- Allowing people to contribute "from head to toe" rather than being used only "from the neck down"
- Understanding processes through examination and analysis
- Building focused teams
- Fostering open, honest, and supportive communication across traditional functional barriers and throughout the sometimes sacrosanct level structure
- Identifying root causes of system deficiencies rather than simply and naturally jumping to conclusions
- Instilling the improvement habit

The idea for the improvement habit was not mine. It came from a conversation I had several years ago with a product assurance manager. He said, "George, what we don't need here is another initiative. What we really need is for all our people, including the managers, to get the improvement habit." When I asked him what he meant, he explained that he believed everyone should get into the habit of constantly improving what they do and never stop.

Finally, CPI will enable and empower people to:

- "Visualize" processes
- Focus on "critical-to-quality" activities in a process
- Significantly improve process output
- Establish an evolutionary improvement system to improve their businesses and help ensure customer satisfaction

- Work together as focused teams
- Build a network of business teams focused on process improvement and customer satisfaction

I recall the reaction of a worker in a consumer electronics plant after her team had diagramed their portion of the manufacturing process. "I've been working here for twenty-two years," she said, "doing basically the same job day in and day out, and I never before knew why I did certain things. Now I can see where I fit and why my job is important. If I don't do my job right, then the next person who gets my work will suffer. Ultimately, we won't make our customers happy, and that's bad for our business."

She had found the link between herself and the customer. The job she had grown to look at as insignificant had taken on new meaning and she knew she had value.

Business Benefits

Now let's turn our attention to the broader topic of business benefits. The objectives of this section are to help you:

- Identify the measurable business benefits which result from implementing the process
- Understand why and how to select an "area opportunity" from a process
- Begin to link broad team plans and goals to business plans and goals.

We will accomplish these objectives by addressing the following subjects:

- What can CPI do for our business?
- The Iceberg Phenomenon
- The Rule of Tens
- Why was our process selected?
- What can our team do for the business?

What Can CPI Do For Our Business?

The benefits of using CPI vary from business to business and from process to process. However, from a broad perspective, CPI

(1) provides a strategy focused on prevention and improvement, and (2) helps build "natural" focused teamwork.

More specifically, the process enables the "natural" focused team to logically, simply, and systematically:

- Reduce scrap and rework
- Reduce cycle time
- Reduce waste
- Reduce inventory
- Provide significant short-term return on investment
- Introduce long-term profit and productivity gains
- Identify and eliminate non-value-adding, nonessential work from processes
- Improve and polish processes worked with daily

Specific examples of team results will be introduced later in the form of case studies and team project summaries.

The Iceberg Phenomenon

Everyone is familiar with the phrase "and that's just the tip of the iceberg," but have you ever thought about what it might mean in the business sense?

The Iceberg Phenomenon is nothing more than recognizing that what you see and measure with respect to losses, scrap, rework, and customer complaint costs is usually only a small and sometimes insignificant part of the total cost impact on a business. If you can accurately account for and measure direct cost drivers and then compare those costs to the indirect costs, you will be able to define the iceberg ratio for your business. Mathematically it would look like this:

$$\text{Iceberg ratio} = \text{indirect costs}/\text{direct costs}$$

Direct costs can be measured and tracked, and are usually accounted for in management reports. The finance and manufacturing divisions are the traditional sources for such data and are the recommended starting points for your search for data in your business.

Indirect costs are those costs that may be difficult to account for, but that you know are real. Some examples are:

- Excess inventory
- Engineering buy-offs
- Material review boards (MRBs)
- Preparation of rework procedures
- Material handling/expediting
- Replanning
- Engineering changes
- Excess capacity
- Marketing concessions
- Lost future orders

Take some time to develop and expand the list for your business and calculate an Iceberg Ratio.

When you have gathered the necessary information and begin to calculate your Iceberg Ratio, you might be interested in what you can expect to find. A ratio of 6 to 1 is not at all unusual. The better you track your losses and account for the true costs associated with such things as customer service, concessions, retraining, expediting, field corrective action, and associated travel expenses, the smaller your ratio will be. Conversely, the fewer records you have and the more loosely you track your indirect costs, the larger your ratio. Some businesses use a complaint accounting system to track these costs. The most important thing to remember is that these costs are real. They are real because they are subtracted from your bottom line, and that realization will get the attention of any finance manager or CEO.

The Rule of Tens

The next subject we will address is called the Rule of Tens. This concept is credited to Dr. Ohno of Toyota. Put in my own words:

Not doing something right the first time costs ten times as much to find and fix each time it escapes to a subsequent stage of handling.

Let's create a scenario to help you fully understand the concept. Suppose you found a design error in a product after it had been delivered to a customer. The number of stages it passed through from design to delivery will indicate how many factors of ten you wasted by not finding and eliminating the problem at its root. For example, if it passed through four stages, then it would cost you approximately a thousand times as much to fix it in the field as it would have cost you in the design stage. The factor stages might look something like this:

Design Effort	Production Cost	Assembly/Test Cost	Field Cost
$100	$1000	$10,000	$100,000

So remember, if you are a design engineer, don't be too anxious to "throw the design over the fence" to production. If you and your design team, which should include manufacturing or production personnel, have not verified the design, it could be very, very costly. It seems that we always have the time to do something the second or third time until we get it right. But now you can see that eventually you won't be able to afford it. In fact, look at what you save by doing it right the first time, even if it takes a little longer to check and verify the design. From the point of view of a general manager, it would be cheaper, more cost effective, and would send the right signals to the business team if shipping dates were missed, as long as that delay meant that it was done right the first time. Think about it.

Why Was Our Process Selected?

This topic is sometimes better known as "Why me?" or "Was it something I said or we did?"

People tend to get paranoid when they, or their work teams, are singled out for a special project. Why? It's usually because something went haywire and the boss is looking for someone to blame. Well, rest easy folks. In the case of the natural work team there is no boss looking for someone to blame because the boss is part of the team. And if something does go wrong within the team he or she will know what went wrong and why and won't go looking for who. In this case, we want to spend some time exploring why certain processes are selected as focal points while others are scheduled to be addressed later. It all comes down to the most critical factors affecting the business and the ability to provide products and services for your customers.

All businesses are composed of a series of processes which are used to provide products and services to customers. They are all important; however, the critical focus changes from time to time based on market needs, competition, and other environmental factors such as corporate expectations and policies.

Based on the "current environmental factors," the top management team identifies the "critical areas of opportunity" for focus and improvement to better meet market needs and fulfill customer expectations, thereby attaining business goals. Just as the natural work teams use certain tools and techniques and follow a given logic to improve their processes, their business management teams use a similar logic and the same tools to select the areas of opportunity for team focus. This allows everyone to speak the same language and enables them to link team plans, goals, and efforts directly to the top-level business plans and goals.

Therefore, it will not be a mystery why management selects a particular CPI team or chooses a "natural" work area as a focus for process improvement. Furthermore, it's not threatening because management is asking what, when, how, and why rather than asking who.

When the system was first implemented in one business, one of the managers reportedly said, "This will help us stop asking the *five who's* and start asking the *five whys.*"

What Can Our CPI Team Do For The Business?

Now that you're over the hurdle of answering the threatening "Why me" question, let's move on to the more pragmatic discovery of what the team can do for the business. In order to help a team understand its charter and contribution to the business, it is necessary to form a clear understanding of the mission of the business.

A clear statement of the business mission must be obtained from top management to ensure that there is no misunderstanding of the basic task. This is the point at which the work begins. Once a mission statement has been clearly formulated, published, and issued to all members of the business, the task of interpreting it begins. It is essential that all levels of management be able to articulate the mission statement in their own words and make the pragmatic link to the process areas they manage. Once that is done, then the natural work teams must take the process one step further and interpret it so that it links to the processes they work with daily. Unless this occurs, the workers will not be able to see the connection between the value of their own jobs and the mission and goals of the business.

It is vitally important that each team in the business know and understand its charter and how it links to the overall mission, plans, and goals. Once that is accomplished, the team can proceed to address simplification and improvement of its own process, knowing that the results will support and have direct impact on overall business plans and goals. That in turn makes it possible for each team member to recognize personal contributed value to the team and to the business.

How Does CPI Work?

Now it is time to share with you the implementation model that has proven to be so successful. My vision of the model may be compared to what I refer to as the "co-op" system of education. When I was in college and graduate school I was always amazed at the direction and interest the co-op students seemed to have. They seemed to have more focus than the rest of us.

As I thought about what made those students different, I discovered one basic underlying and overwhelming factor. The ordinary student simply learned and acquired knowledge, whereas the co-op student experienced the implementation and application of that knowledge. It was this practical application that helped to reinforce the "book learning" and provided guidance toward additional skills and tools required to attain personal and business goals.

Format

Implementation format follows a sequential application:

- Learn a new skill or technique.
- Try in class.
- Experience through application on the job.
- Reinforce through class discussion.

- Continue the cycle.
- Team coaching on the job through successful implementation and initial project completion.
- Congruent training of business coaches to radiate and propagate the process.

The training sequence takes several consecutive weeks using a flexible implementation model. Classes are conducted by a pair of coaches who have first experienced successful teamwork and implementation and are then trained in coaching techniques. The experiential prerequisite builds confidence in the coaches and credibility in the process.

During the initial training, a half day devoted to the use of skills is followed by on-the-job coaching. Later, training is devoted to coaching and continuous use of skills and in some cases the introduction of state-of-the-art technology and a systematic way of deciding when and how to use it. This introduction helps the teams recognize that it isn't necessary to use the latest and greatest technology just because it's there. Rather, they learn to use it when necessary to meet the needs of their customers and the challenges of a complex marketplace.

On-the-job application projects are not dictated by management. Instead, management guides the team by providing areas of opportunity directly associated with their process and linked to the mission, plans, and goals of the business. The team is totally responsible for selecting an application project because no one is more familiar with the process than those people who live with it every day. This builds confidence in the team that management *trusts* them to do the right thing. Because it *empowers and enables* the team to do their job, this decision-making capability *builds the team's ownership* of their process and its improvement.

During the application phase, formal meetings are held to review progress and to see that the plan is being followed. Management attendance and involvement demonstrates commitment to the process. This ensures that the teams are getting active support and not just passive lip service. Formal team presentations are included to (1) report and discuss progress and (2) develop and hone presentation skills. One entire training segment should be devoted to project organization as well as management and presentation skills.

The following cases have been included to help you understand how the process can be implemented and to exhibit the transportability of the tools and techniques into all types of business processes.

Case Study: Electronics Business

The CPI methodology was used effectively by a high-volume electronics manufacturing operation to achieve significant yield improvement in a relatively short time. The plant produced three basic sizes of TV picture tubes in a volume of approximately 7,000 tubes daily.

The techniques were first applied in the matrix room, where black lines are photo-etched onto the surface of the TV screen. The matrix room encompasses a number of sensitive processes which are highly automated. At the time of CPI implementation, the matrix area had an overall yield of approximately 89%. While month-to-month yield variation was experienced, little improvement had been made in the last nine months. Significant machine down time and sudden process aberrations were frequent contributors to the scrap generated in the area. To compound the situation, extra weekend shifts were being used to meet output requirements, while available resources were stretched and time for maintenance activities was minimized. Matrix scrap was detected during a final inspection operation prior to shipment by conveyor to the next process area. Unfortunately, this inspection operation was not 100% effective, resulting in an additional 3% to 4% of scrap in the subsequent process. Additional losses in the final tube test area resulted in significant quality cost losses virtually equal to that accounted for in the matrix room itself.

A multifunctional, multilevel team was assembled. The manager of process engineering was chosen as team sponsor because he was in a position to overcome many of the hurdles and roadblocks the team might encounter. Included on the team were a process engineer, a production supervisor, a machine attendant, and an operator from the chemical mixing room that supplied material to the matrix room. Also, a mechanical technician and a design engineer were chosen as part-time team members. Given the expertise and experience of the group, an excellent source of knowledge concerning both the processes and machines had been assembled.

Team meetings were held once or twice each week. The first meeting dealt with overcoming complacency and switching to an attitude of preventing problems rather than reacting to them. The team established two goals: a 91% yield in matrix and 1.5% scrap in screening. They began their efforts using:

- Process flow diagraming
- Pareto analysis
- Cause and effect relationship analysis
- Storyboarding
- Analytical data charting
- Control charting

Process flow diagraming (see Chapter 2) was used to visualize the matrix room process so the areas critical to quality output could be easily identified and efforts could be properly focused.

As the team built the diagram, their individual opinions and views dissolved and a set of common, refocused team objectives emerged.

An analysis of scrap data showed that machine stoppage was the principal contributor to area scrap, although several process-related defects also contributed. Pareto techniques (see Chapter 3) were used to analyze the significant contributors to machine stoppage. During this exercise, it was discovered that conflicting measurements were being used. While yield was greatly dependent on the number of incidents of stoppage (a measurement the machine attendants and technicians watched closely), the process engineer and production supervisor relied heavily on the accumulated down time data (minutes and hours). This measurement impacted both production load efficiency and line output. By detailing the specific machine operations that contributed to low yield, not load efficiency, a completely different picture of the causes of stoppage was obtained. Control charts were used to track the number of stoppages per machine operation to help set maintenance priority and monitor repair effectiveness.

Additional control charts were established for key process variables. In the past, the data had been collected and recorded in log books by quality control (QC) auditors, machine attendants, and process engineering personnel. Because control charts were posted in a centrally located area, the status of process-focused parameters could be seen by everyone. Communication between people and shifts was dramatically improved. Displaying data on control charts also discouraged tinkering with the process and provided hard data which served as the basis for specific action across the three shifts.

During the first month of operation, scrap resulting from machine stoppage dropped almost 1%. Process scrap did not show any dramatic change. However, improvement in some categories was experienced toward the end of the month. By the end of the second month, the overall yield had increased from 89% to almost 91%. Machine stoppage and two types of process scrap were identified as the principal contributors. Screening room scrap was reduced which demonstrated that the improvement was being seen by the matrix room's customer.

The team continued to search for improvement ideas. A project list was established and specific projects were assigned among team members. In addition, a plan for improved machine preventive maintenance was developed and implemented. This system effectively identified equipment needing weekend maintenance and included a sign-off system for work completion or delay. By the third month, yields improved to record levels, exceeding 92%. Screen room scrap dropped to less than 2.5% and final tube yields improved.

The team celebrated by establishing a new goal. They improved upon the process control plans that they had designed to maintain the progress. Further, they continued to investigate their process for other areas of opportunity. However, even though a new strategy had been adopted, the team was still encumbered by some current ways of doing things, including:

• Management decisions by decree
• Inspection as a sort mechanism
• Shooting-from-the-hip reactions
• Complaining, rather than initiating action

The improvements continued despite these encumbrances and the team learned. Problems that had continually plagued the operation were solved more quickly. The team was even successful in planning for a new design introduction and despite extremely limited resources, equipment modification projects were completed which continued to improve product quality and yield.

Case Study—Procurement Process

CPI START-UP

In mid 1988, a defense-focused business, which we will refer to as DEFCON, began implementation of CPI in the manufacturing and quality areas. The managers of manufacturing and quality assurance jointly sponsored the pilot teams. With the insight and support of their general manager, the process was firmly implanted in the business and became part of the business infrastructure. New operating procedures were created and existing ones changed to reflect the systematic methodology of improvement.

As the initial two teams reported their successes, the message that something different was happening was being transmitted both by the teams and by top management. The process began to spread rapidly to other areas as well. The idea of looking at the work area from a "process" perspective was catching on in an epidemic fashion. Those who protested "We're already doing these things; why do we need something else?" and "Sure it works in manufacturing, but it won't work here" were slowly, but very surely, beginning to understand the power of the simple, structured methodology and were signing up to participate on a team.

IDENTIFYING THE OPPORTUNITIES

As the teams implemented the techniques of CPI, they began to identify other areas of opportunity that occurred "upstream" of their process. They quickly came to the conclusion that if the suppliers to their process did not provide products and services that met or exceeded their requirements, a critical part of their own operations would fail (i.e., they couldn't do their job)! As virtually all the teams made this discovery, it became evident that a procurement process team needed to be selected and trained.

SELECTING THE TEAM

The general "area of opportunity" was identified as procurement. Since procurement covered a broad spectrum, the natural team that was formed contained a mix of people both with acquisition experience and without. The manager of compliance and administration was designated team sponsor, based on his experience and expertise. Ad hoc members were also invited, to give the team full ownership of the process. Once the team was formed, formal training began, combined with coaching to implement the tools and techniques on the job.

GETTING STARTED

During the first two training and coaching sessions, the team discovered why the procurement process was critical to the business. As the sponsoring manager explained, "In our business approximately 50% of the goods and services required for production flow through purchasing. We can make a major and direct impact because every dollar saved in the purchasing process goes directly to the bottom line. With the internal pressure on dealing with low-cost suppliers, it was the obvious place to start.

"Besides, it is a well known and common perception that everyone is frustrated with the amount of time it takes to process material requests."

He reported that the team initially got off to a false start. The procurement process was too broad and all-inclusive, the team did not stringently follow the process steps, and they got wrapped up in some nonessentials. They got back on track, however, by starting to work on something they could "get their arms around." Instead of tackling the entire process, they broke it down into four pieces which they referred to as cycles:

1. Material request cycle
2. Purchase order cycle
3. Supplier manufacturing cycle
4. Delivery cycle

ANALYZING THE PROCESS

Recognizing that the material request (MR) cycle was perceived to be a major roadblock by most people who relied on the purchasing operation, the team decided this would be their starting point. The MR cycle also happened to be the first part of the procurement process that anyone had to contend with.

As part of their training, the team learned how to display the MR process visually through process flow diagraming (PFD). This technique allowed them to synthesize their thoughts and identify the "hot points." According to the sponsoring manager, "Many of the team members thought they understood the process but they were unable to put it into words. When we put it into pictures, however, it was transformed into a common language that we could all understand. It drove common thinking. Once the process was diagramed, the team comments went from 'Boy, I don't know what we're going to do, this looks impossible!' to 'Hey, if we fix this one little thing and then fix another little thing, the sum of the parts will exceed the whole!' "

At this point the team really began to function as a unit. Ad hoc team members from the information technology, finance, and quality assurance organizations, contributed an internal customer or supplier perspective and the team began to believe that they could solve their problems.

During the brainstorming and problem-solving sessions, one team member was overheard to say: "You know, I thought of this ten years ago but no one listened to me. Now we can do something about it." And another concluded, "This is great! We should have done it years ago!"

FOCUSING ON CRITICAL PROCESS ELEMENTS

The next training session helped the team decide what was critical. Tools and techniques were included to help prioritize information gathered from the process and decide what to work on first, and to maintain focus on the "what" and the "why" and avoid looking for the "who." To begin, the team performed a "re's" analysis. This led them through the rigor of defining all the parts of the MR process that began with the prefix "re." They concluded that the most wasteful part of their process was probably anything that had to be done more than once. Having performed the analysis, the team narrowed their list to the top three:

- Reject
- Re-approve
- Re-input

Using all the information gathered, they were able to prepare a clear problem statement which would become the basis for process analysis:

The material request cycle time appears to be excessive.

The wording was chosen based on internal "customer" perception. The next task was to isolate the principal causes of the problem. To do this, they constructed a structure tree. This tool brought focus to: (1) the single system for processing all MRs and (2) the abundance of redundant approvals.

LISTENING TO THE PROCESS

During the next meeting, the team was coached in the technique of "listening" to their process. This helped them identify and analyze available data to (1) quantify the length of the MR cycle, and (2) identify the place to begin improving the process.

When they performed a statistical analysis of the available data, it was clear that the cycle was taking too long. By plotting the total number of MRs as a function of the number of days in the cycle, the team found that the average time to process an MR was ten days. They got similar results when they sampled the data. The sponsoring manager reported: "It was fascinating how accurate the data was. I'm not talking about thousands of samples. We took samples from fifty to one hundred lot sizes and they proved to be very accurate. For example, we picked purchase orders that were under $150 as a subset of the entire purchasing process. Then we looked at the cycle time from the time when the initiating signature was placed on the MR to the time the buyer received it."

During the next training session, the team was introduced to "interpretation and control." They discovered how to apply appropriate charts to any process. They were able to select the proper control chart to display and interpret process data. During the coaching session, data from the MR process was plotted on this chart.

By using the information from the structure tree and the PFD, they were able to analyze the process to determine which steps did not add value and which steps were taking the longest time to execute. As you will see, the PFD and available data led to some surprising results.

IMPROVING THE PROCESS

The team turned to customer requirements and expectations as standards of measurement to determine which steps added the least value. One member explained: "One thing that everyone in our business has on his or her mind is something called compliance. [Compliance in this sense means strict adherence to government regulations and guidelines.] When we looked at the controlling steps of the MR process, we found one of them was an approval from Finance on any overhead MR.

"We looked at that step in light of what people are allowed to spend on their expense reports, with petty cash, and with other daily transactions, and we realized we were overcontrolling the process. When we asked 'Why are we controlling this to this level?' no one was really quite sure."

It became obvious from the detailed analysis that the control was costing more than it was adding value. Furthermore, the control was being levied by DEFCON's finance operation. So the team decided to visit the finance manager.

When he reviewed the process flow diagram and the control chart, the manager quickly recognized that the logical thing to do was to eliminate the approval step. In fact, he was pleased that the team had found a way to reduce the amount of work his people had to do that was not adding value to the business.

RESULTS

The following specific results were seen nine weeks after beginning training and application.

- MR cycle time was reduced from ten days to three days.
- The purchasing function was no longer seen as a roadblock.
- The finance department reduced its work load.
- Finance also eliminated a non-value-added approval step.

When asked for his perspective on the improvement process, the sponsoring manager shared the following:

When we began, the MR process was taking ten days; that cycle is now three days for a material request against overhead under $150. We have not only reduced the cycle time, but also have precipitated a change in attitude toward the purchasing function. It was seen as very much a roadblock for no good reason. We're demonstrating that we are really trying to change that image.

A big spin-off from this effort was that other people came forward with other changes. They began to think that, golly, someone had a good idea and they actually implemented it. If I have a good idea, I'm going to see if they will do it for me.

The benefit from CPI is not merely the CPI "process." It is very important to understand that there is a CPI attitude. It is the attitude change at this point that is probably producing the greatest results.

People are beginning to question *why* they do things. I have several clerks that work for me. They asked why they have to distribute 8,000 pages of weekly reports. We decided there is really no reason and cut the volume to 3,500 sheets of paper almost overnight.

I believe the finance operations agreement to eliminate the non-value-adding approvals sent the right signal that we are supporting CPI and that many other things can be done.

BUSINESS RESULTS

DEFCON's manufacturing and quality assurance managers were asked to comment on the broader business benefits of using the CPI process after the first year of training and implementation.

The quality manager's response was captured from an interview printed in the local works newspaper:

> Last July we were not meeting the scheduled production rate for a major customer. Once the CPI teams got rolling, however, we were not only able to get our heads above water by January but we were also able to stay there. We got the rate up because CPI helped point out how to do things faster and better. Even with the increased production rate, we were able to significantly reduce the defect rate. We would not have managed that without CPI.

The manager of manufacturing had these comments:

> One of the greatest concerns a manufacturing manager has is a significant production rate increase. Over the past year we increased our production from seven to eight units per month

to a high of seventy to eighty units per month. I do not believe we would have been able to accomplish that without CPI.

Furthermore, without the process we probably would not have made the rate in the time allotted. That could have severely jeopardized our position with our customer, possibly resulting in the loss of the contract.

Institutionalization of CPI

Changes and improvements made by the procurement process team were institutionalized in the business by (1) changing the computer system, and (2) rewriting departmental procedures to reflect the changes.

Proof that institutionalization of the process is indeed taking place and is growing was provided by the team sponsoring manager:

> We have rewritten departmental procedures and it is fascinating how change and new and faster ways are being accepted by top management. They are thrilled. Feedback from top management that says, "That was a good thing to do. Thank you. Keep it up!" is worth more than many other things that could be done.
>
> In the past we frequently let a process operate just because it always had, without really understanding what the process consisted of. It was just the mysterious "system," like the word "they." Now, we are rewriting overall procedures, using much of the same mindset, in eliminating non-value-adding tasks by understanding the process first and then the actual requirement of the process.

As a result of team efforts and the message sent by management that things are indeed different, teams have continued to identify new areas of opportunity for themselves as well as for new teams. Perpetuation has been rooted in team ownership of the business processes. DEFCON provides an excellent model for others to follow.

CPI Implementation Flow Chart

Remembering your definition of a process: it is a series of steps which, when executed in some logical order, deliver an output.

Like any other process, there is a certain logic to be used to implement CPI. Some general steps have been captured for your use and reference in Figure 1–1.

By using this flow chart as a guideline and reminder you and your team will be able to:

- Visualize your process
- Identify and eliminate root causes of problems
- Identify and eliminate non-value-adding work from your process
- Test process capabilities against customer requirements
- Establish and maintain process control
- Prepare and document operating procedures for the in-control process
- Continuously improve the process
- Manage your work area by being process focused and aware of the bottom line

Teams find this logic chart very useful to track progress through the implementation steps. Posting the chart in the work area will help keep your team on track and able to follow all the sequential steps to ensure that they don't jump to conclusions. C-T-Q on the flow chart refers to critical-to-quality, i.e., those factors critical to meeting customer needs and expectations.

Tools and Techniques

To move from the philosophical into practical application we need tools and techniques. The objectives of this section will be to define two distinct problem-solving techniques and then introduce you to, or reaquaint you with, several simple tools. Before going any further, however, I want to warn you not to expect any dramatic revelation, because you probably won't find anything new. However, you may well discover a lot of the things that you have used from time to time to solve problems. As we proceed you will find out how these tools are systematically linked together.

When CPI was first introduced to the manager of manufacturing referred to in the previous case study, he said, "This is the first time I've seen all the things I've ever used to solve problems

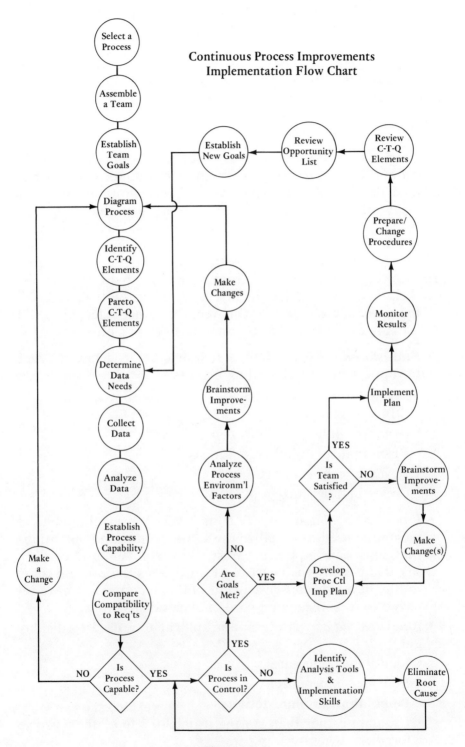

**Continuous Process Improvements
Implementation Flow Chart**

Figure 1–1

REPRINTED BY PERMISSION OF GENERAL ELECTRIC.

that actually worked all gathered together in one spot. Here they are linked so you can logically follow from one step to the next. This is great!"

Problem-solving Techniques

Two basic types of techniques are used to solve problems, *judgmental* and *analytical*. The judgmental technique is used when detailed data is not available; analytical techniques are used when quantifiable information and data are available. Judgmental techniques are used to get the process started by helping the team exercise their thought process and come to consensus on where to begin and what to do. The analytical techniques are introduced to enable the team to dialogue with the process and help verify initial judgments. By linking the two, you will see the process come to life. One team member referred to CPI as "a living organism" that became part of their business.

- *Brainstorming* is a judgmental tool used to generate ideas to support the storyboarding process.
- *Storyboarding* in turn is used to:
  - Stimulate creativity
  - Organize judgmental problem solving
  - Visually display individual ideas
  - Develop team consensus
  - Create and organize a plan

- *Process flow diagraming* (*PFD*) is a very powerful analytical technique used to visualize the steps, events, and operations that constitute a process. Most team members and coaches say this is truly the heart of CPI. It makes the process come to life, develops consensus, and builds teamwork. I have referred to it as the spinal cord or skeletal structure.
- *Analytical data charting* is a graphical tool used to display data to:
  - Identify problem areas
  - Interpret information
  - Pinpoint and isolate activity
  - Use data rather than storing it until it's too late or you've forgotten where you put it.

- *Control charting* is a simple, but very powerful tool used to:
  - Let you dialogue with your process
  - Recognize trends
  - Avoid producing bad products or services
  - Prevent problems rather than react to them after it's too late

Each of these tools and techniques will be introduced sequentially so you will see how they work individually and how they fit together to simplify and improve the way you and your team perform your daily tasks.

Brainstorming

Now let's look into brainstorming in detail. The objectives of this exploration are:

- To introduce you to or reacquaint you with the technique of brainstorming
- To provide you with some basic questions used in the technique
- To enable you to experience the effectiveness and power of brainstorming

Definitions

Webster offers the following definitions for your consideration:

Brain: The center of thought.

Storm: An outburst of emotion.

Brainstorming: The unrestrained offering of ideas or suggestions by all members of a conference to seek solutions to problems.

When used in the total process context, brainstorming stimulates the thought process and is a critical part of storyboarding. Discussion or dialogue is discouraged in a brainstorming session because it gets people off track or kills ideas. It is essential that an open, supportive environment be maintained to ensure the success of a session. This is done by observing and enforcing all the basic CPI ground rules presented at the beginning of the chapter.

When brainstorming is properly done, people find they can "piggyback" off the ideas of others and develop team synergy and spontaneity that they would not normally experience.

Questions used to stimulate brainstorming

To ensure the success of a brainstorming session there are four basic questions you want to remember and two you want to avoid. To finish this thought on a positive note, let's begin with the two *you must avoid at all cost:* Why? and Who? They should not be used because they are probing and threatening. "Why?" should be reserved until you are analyzing a problem to find the root cause. At that point you will be encouraged to use it relentlessly. But for now, forget that it exists. As for the big "Who," I suggest you avoid that unless you are interrogating your kids. And, from the lessons learned by parenting three children, I'm not too sure what value it has in that environment, either.

The questions that have real value in this process are:

• What?
• Where?
• When?
• How much?

Storyboarding

The objectives of this section are to:

• Familiarize or reintroduce you to the technique of storyboard-
  ing
• Illustrate the power of this tool
• Provide you with easy-to-follow steps to run your own success-
  ful storyboarding sessions
• Allow you to experience the process through an exercise
• Recognize the links between brainstorming and this unique
  tool

To accomplish these objectives we will be addressing the following topics:

• What is storyboarding?
• What is needed to run a storyboarding session?

- Who is involved?
- How does a session really work?
- Possible storyboard layout
- Storyboarding steps

What Is Storyboarding?

Storyboarding has been around for a long time. According to an Italian friend of mine Michelangelo was the first to use the process in the Sistine Chapel. More recently its origin has been credited to the late Walt Disney as the process he used to put the words and music together for his cartoons.

No matter who really began the process or how it spread, it has become a very powerful technique when properly linked with a few other problem-solving tools.

I have chosen to define *storyboarding* as follows:

A technique used to organize logically and display visually a plan to solve a problem.

As you use the technique and begin to experience its unexpected advantages, you will find more opportunities to put it to work. In fact, you will wonder how you ever got along without it.

What Is Needed to Run a Storyboard Session?

The essential elements required to run a storyboarding session are austere, but focused. The list that follows will give you an opportunity to examine the elements necessary for a successful session. You are invited and encouraged to find and modify those pieces you find necessary to fit your requirements.

1. First, you need five to seven people to realize the controlled spontaneity.
2. You need a comfortable meeting room.
3. Be sure you have no interruptions. Put "Do Not Disturb" sign on the door.
4. You must have clear walls to display ideas. (Corkboard or the equivalent is preferred.) A portable board is a good idea if you will need to change your meeting place, and because you can transport it to your work area to display your process.

5. You will need cards in multiple sizes and different colors. Self-adhering note pads have been creatively used.
6. Pins or adhesive are required to attach the cards to the wall, unless they are self-adhering.
7. Dark marking pens will be needed to write on the cards. The large style generally used for flip chart work is recommended. Avoid using the type that emits a strong odor because you will be working in a closed area for an extended period of time.

Who Is Involved?

There are three roles to be filled to make the process work.

- *Facilitator:* This individual asks questions to generate ideas, keeps the session on track, maintains the proper environment, and breaks ties.
- *Pinner:* This person transfers the completed cards to the wall. This role should be rotated among the team members.
- *Writers:* These people generate and call out ideas. As the ideas are called out, they are recorded on cards and then handed to the pinner for display.

You should be cautioned that even though storyboarding is fun and stimulating, it can be very draining. Therefore, it is recommended that you schedule appropriate breaks and have refreshments readily available.

How Does a Session Really Work?

The session begins with a clear statement of the problem to be addressed and the objectives to be accomplished. Unless you have clear, concise objectives, the session will lack direction and will become an exercise in futility.

Once the objectives are clearly stated, it is important to identify why the problem must be solved. This step involves compiling a list of benefits that would be expected as a result of resolving the situation at hand. It is suggested that benefits be clearly identified for:

- Customers, both internal and external
- The business
- The team

As ideas are generated and displayed, logical groupings will appear. When this happens, you should categorize them accordingly and develop appropriate headings. It is very important that you do not force topic headings. Experience shows that ideas from the brainstorming process often create more effective topic headings than you might otherwise consider. Besides, predetermined topics may curtail ideas and stifle spontaneity.

Possible Storyboard Layout

A storyboard can take on just about any shape imaginable. The free form and flexibility of the process make it fun and creative. Figure 1–2 shows just one possibility for a layout.

Well-formulated and active storyboards are sometimes creatively color coded so project status can be quickly and easily reviewed. For example, some teams have chosen to use red cards to signify overdue items and green to illustrate completion. Creating your own system is fun and helps build team ownership of the process.

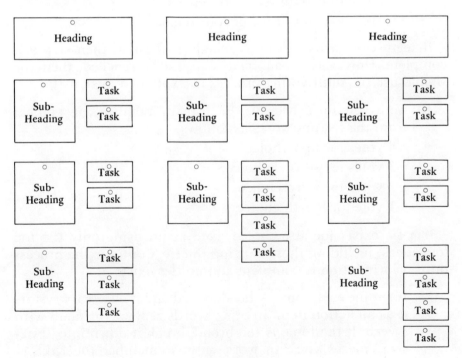

Figure 1–2

Storyboarding Steps

Let's list the storyboarding events in chronological order for future reference. You may find it helpful to post a copy of the list to help keep your team on track.

1. State the problem.
2. Develop the purpose.
3. List the benefits of solving the problem.
4. Identify headers if appropriate. Otherwise, let the brainstorming results generate the topics.
5. Brainstorm and post all ideas.

Once the board is filled or ideas begin to dry up, take time to clean up the board by eliminating redundancies and by grouping cards as naturally as possible. Remember not to force anything.

6. Review each card to ensure the team agrees on its meaning.
7. Clarify and rewrite the cards if necessary.
8. Eliminate irrelevant or redundant cards. Cards may be removed *only* with team consensus.
9. Identify your top three or four ideas.

If team consensus can be reached on the list, then step 9 is complete. However, if consensus can not be reached, then you should use the multivoting process as explained in step 10.

10. Multivote for consensus. Each team member selects ideas from the list and votes as follows:
    - 4 votes for first choice
    - 3 votes for second choice
    - 2 votes for third choice
    - 1 vote for fourth choice

If a tie exists for any choice, vote again using only the top four ideas, including those causing the tie. Continue the process until prioritization is complete and no ties exist.

11. Examine each topic or header card and if necessary restate it as an action item. In other words replace the noun with a verb. If the topic is too broad, break it down into "bite-size" pieces you can work with. Remember the K.I.S.S. rule.

12. If subtier actions are necessary, post them under the header card. If there isn't enough room, use an adjacent space and make the link with color coded cards, string, yarn, or numbers on the cards. Use your imagination and whatever tools you have on hand.

13. Assign a completion date to each appropriate item. It's important that the person responsible for the item agrees with the date.

14. Post dates and the name of the responsible person on either side of the action card. Should responsibilities or dates change, the cards should be adjusted accordingly to maintain the accuracy of the board.

15. Sequence action items by date. This step is optional. It does require additional effort to move cards around on the board, but ordering events chronologically helps manage the implementation and completion of the projects.

16. As items are completed or become overdue, it is recommended that a color coding system be used to indicate project status, such as green for complete and red for overdue.

Why Does CPI Work?

I suppose you're still wondering what makes this overall process different from other initiatives, why it works? With that question in mind, the objectives of this section are:

- To help you understand why CPI is not "business as usual"
- To distinguish clearly the differences between a "program" and a "process"
- To display the power and synergy of organized, skilled, and trained teamwork

To fulfill these objectives, we will address the following topics:

- Why programs fail
- Teamwork
- Ownership
- Team goals
- Real time application
- What do we absorb or retain?

Why Programs Fail

It seems we can always remember the names of programs that got started with some good idea in mind, but fizzled out after a while. Understanding why they failed and recognizing some common attributes can help you avoid similar pitfalls.

"Programs" usually are associated with kick-offs, hype, slogans, bells and whistles, and have little direct tie to business plans and goals. Sometimes they form a weak tie-in with the business mission if a well articulated mission statement exists. In general, programs usually leave you feeling that "All I have to do is wait this one out. When it dies, we'll be back to business as usual until another bright idea comes along." Sound familiar?

Teamwork

Webster's *New World Dictionary* defines *teamwork* as follows:

Joint action by a group of people, in which individual interests are subordinated to group unity and efficiency; coordinated effort, as of an athletic team.

One of the biggest problems I have run into when addressing this topic is that people really have trouble grasping the concept of teamwork. They seem to think they know what it is and they also seem to know the value of it. And people often think that they are operating as a team because they consider themselves good team players. However, there is more to it than that.

WHO ARE THE REAL TEAM MEMBERS?

The real working team consists of all those people from a product-related and/or process-related work area who are focused on attaining common goals. The most effective teams are composed of four to six basic members with ad hoc members added and changed as indicated by the process or dictated by the goals.

A typical generic team may look something like this:

• Sponsoring manager
• Coach-in-training
• Natural team member
• Natural team member

- Natural team member
- Ad hoc member
- Ad hoc member

Once the natural team is identified, it remains intact, functional, and permanent. However, individuals and focus may change over time. Some cross-functional teams have been put together for a specific purpose and then disbanded after they attained their goals. But since part of their cross-functional activity was to identify opportunities for natural teams, after the team was disbanded, its members helped spawn new teams, so the process lived on.

THE ROLE OF EACH TEAM MEMBER

Each team member is expected to:

- Be supportive
- Contribute
- Be creative
- Add value

Additionally, the sponsoring manager has some responsibilities the others do not. He or she must:

- Build bridges
- Remove obstacles
- Obtain and allocate resources
- Know when to *lead*
- Know when to *follow*
- Know when to *get out of the way* and allow team members to do their job
- Recognize and reward team accomplishments
- Turn mundane, unproductive staff meetings into productive and proactive team meetings.

The ad hoc team members have the added responsibility to:

- Provide outside resources that are otherwise missing from the "natural" team
- Give the team a view of their activity from the eyes of a customer or supplier
- Help ensure the team has complete ownership of the process

Coaches-in-training are unique because they are not only operating team members but they have also been singled out to continue the training and radiation of the process. Therefore, they should be able to:

- Transfer expertise and ownership from other coaches and the written materials to your business
- Support growth and radiation of the process
- Help groom new coaches
- Act as change agents to make CPI a part of the daily work life

Ownership

The word ownership has been used freely and without explanation thus far. For this reason, and because you and your team cannot accomplish anything without having ownership, it's necessary that I share with you how to perform the test for it.

The ownership test was devised after many years of experiencing success and failure and recognizing some simple, but very key elements associated with those successes and failures. The test will help ensure that you have all resources and requirements necessary to be successful in meeting your goals.

There are five criteria:

- *Responsibility* to do the job
- *Authority* to make decisions
- *Skills* to meet the challenge
- *Accountability* to complete the task according to plan and schedule
- *Recognition* of what the team has and plans to do

Once the process you will be focusing on has been identified, the ownership test can be used to make sure your team has the necessary resources to truly own the process. The test must be applied continuously to determine validity of current team composition and the requirements for ad hoc members.

Team Goals

Team goals are a natural outgrowth of the goals of the individuals on the team. As individuals, each person has an opinion of what is important and what should be done. We are all different, so of course personal goals differ. As a team it is most important to identify a set of congruent goals that can be embraced as a team. The importance of this cannot be stressed enough, because unless a team pulls together toward a common goal, the team will be pulled apart by the individuals trying to attain their own pet goals.

Webster defines a *goal* as:

An object or end that one strives to attain.

I like to think about a goal as:

A vision of what you want to happen.

If you can see it, you can accomplish it, and I've found that if you can turn a common team goal into a vision of what the team wants to accomplish, then it will happen.

Following my definition of a personal goal, I like to think of a team goal as:

A common vision held by a group of individuals.

Real Time Application

As I mentioned earlier, the co-op technique of learning led me to believe that it had far-reaching value extending beyond the educational world. Believing that, the co-op philosophy was used to translate classroom education into experiential real time application.

Experience with the technique has proven that immediate meaningful application of skills increases retention. It also illustrates the benefits of using the skills in the work place.

I recall my wife recounting her experiences in training to be a registered nurse. The students were first introduced to a new patient care technique in the classroom, but this was immediately followed by practice under the guidance of an experienced nurse or doctor. Students were advised of the benefits of administering the technique as illustrated and practiced, and were warned about the consequences of applying an unauthorized or unproven technique. In the medical field there is no room for error and the results are often irreversible. If we were to act with similar care and forethought in the business world, we could avoid many of the errors we carelessly make and reap more of the rewards our customers can provide in the form of repeat and new business.

What Do We Absorb or Retain?

We learn by reinforcing what we have been taught or through self-discovery. The degree of retention is a function of our involvement. I borrowed the following information from a General Electric training brochure developed in 1986. I searched for the origin of the information but was unable to locate it to give proper recognition. In any event, the results of the many teams seem to indicate that we absorb or retain:

- 10% of what we read
- 20% of what we hear
- 30% of what we see
- 50% of what we hear and see
- 70% of what we say ourselves
- 90% of what we do ourselves

Without statistical data to support my conclusion, but after watching teams work together through learning and implementa-

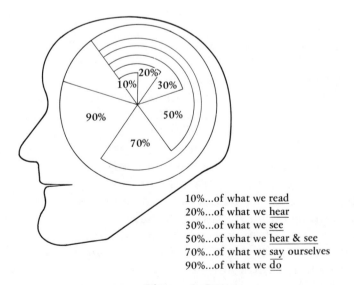

10%...of what we read
20%...of what we hear
30%...of what we see
50%...of what we hear & see
70%...of what we say ourselves
90%...of what we do

Figure 1–3

REPRINTED BY PERMISSION OF GENERAL ELECTRIC.

tion of the process, I would expect that the retention and absorption spectrum is stretched above the 90% level. A graphical illustration of this discussion is shown in Figure 1–3. Teams have found it helpful to post this diagram in an obvious location as a reminder and reinforcement. Our three children have found the concept quite useful in high school and college. They were able to devise their own form of team learning. They found that by teaching each other the concepts they knew individually, they could transfer their knowledge, thereby both helping each other and also reinforcing their own understanding and application of a new concept or technique.

What Makes CPI Continuous?

Before you get to your first Real Time Application Assignment, there is one last item to address. That is the topic of what makes CPI continuous.

The objectives of this discussion are fourfold:

- To identify the key ingredients required to make CPI continuous
- To help you better understand your role and the role of the other team members
- To introduce the improvement habit
- To begin formulation of team meetings and development of productive meeting habits

To accomplish these objectives we will address:

- Commitment
- "Natural" teamwork
- Team planning
- Linking your process to business plans and goals
- Making meetings productive
- The improvement habit
- Proof that it works
- Team identification

Commitment

CPI will work only when each and every individual makes a personal commitment to:

- Personally seek improvement
- Support team goals
- Support and embrace the ground rules
- Fulfill customer expectations
- Make the methodology a way of life

Each person must *want* to make it work. It seems there is always "one in every crowd" who tries to make life difficult for those around them. I've found that these people take the longest time to buy in but they end up being some of the staunchest supporters. These are the "doubting Thomases" who must be led, shown, and convinced every step of the way. Experience has shown that they always come around. One of my colleagues, Paula Wright, loves to tell the story about a middle-level manager who dominated one initial training session. He loudly complained that the training was too slow, too fundamental, and an obvious waste of time. After being involved in the initial part of the process, he openly confessed that he had grossly misinterpreted the power of the simplicity and logic he initially saw. He became, and still remains, one of the pillars of CPI in that business.

I had a similar experience early on with a quality assurance manager. He had always questioned and, to my chagrin, constantly tested the contributed value of training and education. Once he convinced himself beyond any shadow of doubt that the process had value, he became a sponsor for the initial business implementation. After each semester of training, a meeting was held to give all teams the opportunity to present their initial results and their plans for continuing their improvement activity. At the meeting following the third semester of training, he publicly announced his support and commitment to the process in front of an audience of approximately 120 people which included the customer. The following was printed in the local newspaper:

"CPI," says the manager of Quality Assurance and Test, "is by far the best and most useful tool I've ever seen. Almost everyone who has worked with it will say the same thing."

"The first two rounds had us initially using it on new processes," he explained. "Now we're digging into processes as old as the Department. Now, when you want to try something new, it's like making a revision to the Bible."

It takes commitment like this from all levels of management and from the team members alike to make CPI truly a continuous process. As you progress through the text, you will be introduced to additional examples to help reinforce in your own mind that CPI works and to show you what it takes to make it happen.

"Natural" Teamwork

You will recall when we discussed who the real team members were, we identified generic titles and described the roles and activities associated with each. Those people who work together each day are best suited to identify, assess, and address the processes they use to deliver products and services to their customers. The innate power of "natural teamwork" is generated when these individuals join together in a common work area and with a set of common objectives linked to easily articulated and well-understood business goals. This power far surpasses the results of individual efforts or the reactive efforts of unfocused teams. Your personal experience will help reinforce this possibly unexpected result.

Team Planning

Planning is almost a sacred event to a team. If you don't plan your strategy effectively, you cannot execute with any anticipation or expectation of positive results.

Any of you who do woodworking will understand the phrase, "measure twice and cut once." Proper planning helps avoid errors and provides attainable and trackable events in your problem-solving process.

Team planning is a fundamental requirement for attainment of team goals. It takes a lot of effort to ensure plans are congruent and you have team buy-in. Execution of a well-organized team plan which continuously focuses attention on streamlining and improving areas critical to your business will help assure continuation of CPI. In short, if continuation is part of the planning process, then CPI will be continuous.

Linking Your Process to Business Plans and Goals

Each team member and each team must be able to see the natural link between process team plans and goals and the top-level plans and goals of the business. If they are properly linked and aligned, then the focus will be common and the contribution of the team to the business can be articulated. It is at this juncture that this methodology can become part of the business infrastructure. Your earlier experience with articulating the mission statement of your business and understanding the plans and goals of your management team are the links I refer to. As you procede with the implementation process, the importance of this activity will gain more clarity and will be reinforced.

Making Meetings Productive

I'm sure you will agree that a tremendous amount of time is wasted in meetings. You would also agree that from time to time you have attended meetings that yielded positive results. It is the objective of this subsection to give you the tools to help make your team meetings as productive as possible.

The following guidelines are commonsense steps you should follow when preparing for, and when conducting a meeting. Modify the steps as necessary to suit your particular needs.

1. Know what you are going to do before you get to the meeting.
2. Come to every meeting prepared with previous commitments completed on schedule.
3. Begin on time.
4. Post agenda and time schedule at the beginning of each meeting.
5. Distribute copies of the action item list from the previous meeting.
6. Keep meeting on track and on schedule.
7. Record action items and responsibility. Distribute and post with your process flow diagram.
8. Prepare a plan and agenda for the next meeting. Determine meeting length in accordance with the agenda. *Plan ahead!*
9. End on time.

An unstructured, free-flowing meeting may also be unproductive. A well-managed meeting, where each individual has assigned roles and responsibilities, is more likely to proceed smoothly and without confusion.

Role	Responsibility
* Meeting leader (selected by team)	* Preside over the meeting Post productive planner and use it to keep meeting on track
* Timer (selected by team)	* Keep meeting on schedule. (Use of horn, bell, whistle, or marshmallows can be fun and effective. Use your imagination and have fun.)
* Recorder (selected by team)	* Record action items as they are identified Update items as completed Prepare productive planner for next meeting
* Team members	* Be on time * Come prepared * Keep on track * Keep on schedule * Maintain positive environment * Support leader
* Special invitees	* Listen * Support team needs

The Improvement Habit

There are many ways to accomplish change. However, to effect a fundamental change in the way people think and act is not easy and cannot be achieved in a short time. It takes us many years to become the people we are and to develop the habits that are totally ours. Therefore changing such patterns requires a common focal point, something that everyone involved with can rally around and constantly remain attached to, and this will take time.

Earlier, I recounted conversation with a product assurance manager about the difficulties he encountered in trying to accomplish change in his organization. He suggested that people needed the "improvement habit." The idea stuck, and the sequential steps he outlined have become synonymous with CPI:

- Plan
- Act
- Verify
- Institutionalize

The improvement habit simply replaces individual procrastination with a "we-can-find-a-better-way!" team attitude.

When the process was being introduced into another business one manager offered the following observation, one not peculiar to that business alone:

> "Plan, act, verify, and institutionalize" is a great idea. We can make it happen, but it's going to take a lot of effort because what we do now is plan, then we talk about it, then we procrastinate, and finally we have to cover our rears because we never took the time to do what we initially set out to do.

Continuous application of the improvement habit will enable your team to improve the processes in their "natural" work area on an ongoing basis. The graphical representation of the improvement habit is shown in the form of a wheel in Figure 1–4. It illustrates the unending nature of CPI and provides a simple picture to associate with the process. This is reproduced with the consent of GE.

Proof That It Works

Proof that CPI really works comes in testimonials from people using it and in some impressive bottom-line results. Several businesses reported $35 million in cumulative savings from eliminating unnecessary and nonproductive work during the first two years after CPI was introduced. Three testimonials by managers from those businesses are included for your information and as a baseline to test and gauge your progress.

When asked, "Does CPI have a positive effect on cost," the manager of quality and test previously quoted replied:

> As a matter of fact it addresses what's called the "Iceberg Effect."
>
> Little mistakes, let's face it, cost big dollars in the number of reports generated to correct them . . . the actions that have to be taken to turn them around.

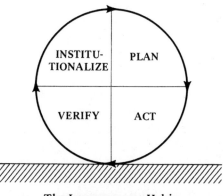

The Improvement Habit

Figure 1–4

REPRINTED BY PERMISSION OF GENERAL ELECTRIC.

That's why, if you save a buck through CPI, you're really saving six dollars or more through the hidden costs that will not be chalked up, thanks to the problem you've eliminated.

When asked to comment on the value of CPI, a manager of manufacturing engineering responded:

If you accept the "Iceberg Effect" of every dollar saved multiplying itself six times or better, that could amount to over $1 million. We think that's conservative. We can see CPI's demonstrated cost savings in shop and support costs.

The manager of production engineering from the electronics business referred to in the earlier case study had these comments:

In the matrix and screening area we obtained a 5% yield improvement in combined efficiency. In addition, we hit a twenty-two-year high in matrix efficiency and we never did that before. Involvement of people who used to just sit back and watch, plus these results, is proof that it's working.

The following project summaries will give you an idea of the various types of improvement projects teams chose. Your team will have an opportunity to make a similar summary after your initial project has been completed. The summary sheet gives you an idea of the expectations that need to be fulfilled and the progression of steps required to complete a project.

Project Summary A

TEAM FOCUS:

Supplier process

AREA OF OPPORTUNITY:

This team was established to address the process used to control suppliers. Vendor-supplied hardware had become the largest single item of cost on major contracts. Adequate control of suppliers was essential to meet management objectives.

PROBLEM STATEMENT:

The team identified the time delay of issuing design changes as the first area they would address. Through process flow diagraming and statistical data analysis, they arrived at a problem statement:

It takes four to six weeks for an issued alteration notice (AN) to get to our supplier base.

ACTION PLAN:

Analyzing the process flow diagram revealed that most of the steps were redundant when compared with the "AN" approval process. A cause and effect analysis showed that much time was lost due to delays in the internal mail system. The team developed a new process flow and reduced the number of steps from 106 to 7. This flow required electronic sign-off and the co-location of some support organizations, both of which were being planned. The team was able to ensure their requirements were included as part of the overall plan.

VERIFICATION OF RESULTS:

The team conducted a timing study to determine the effectiveness of the changes. The new procedure reduced the "AN" cycle from four to six weeks to two days. Relocation of support units continues.

INSTITUTIONALIZATION PROCESS:

Training for the support organization was implemented concurrently. Procedures were updated to reflect the new process flow and relocation of support units continues.

CONTINUING ACTIONS:

The team is identifying other areas of improvement with the new business-wide sourcing organization.

Project Summary B

TEAM FOCUS:

Shop Tooling and Setup

AREA OF OPPORTUNITY:

This was a natural work team responsible for shop tooling in a business that performs machining on virtually all major commodities they deliver. The setup and teardown of tooling has a direct effect on shop productivity.

PROBLEM STATEMENT:

The team's first project dealt with delays, not defects. After performing a statistical analysis of setup time, they arrived at the following problem statement:

Approximately one-third of the time to set up a job is wasted because fixtures, gauges, tools, and hardware are not available to operators.

ACTION PLAN:

The process flow diagram indicated a number of delays and "re's" in the setup cycle. A detailed structure tree identified 32 separate root causes. It was discovered that most of the causes could be eliminated by creating a central storage area where all fixtures, gauges, and tools could be organized in sequential order. The team established a detailed plan to implement this system within four weeks.

VERIFICATION OF RESULTS:

Since the team started measuring and tracking setup time, only minor improvement was realized. The plan to establish a new system was implemented with estimated savings of 1,700 hours per year.

INSTITUTIONALIZATION PROCESS:

The new system was documented and operator training was implemented. A monthly analysis of setup time was established to verify corrective action.

CONTINUING ACTIONS:

The team continued to address other setup issues including universal fixturing. In addition, they initiated a team to evaluate inspection procedures and fixtures and the way they are used.

Project Summary C

TEAM FOCUS:

Plastics and Bond Shop

AREA OF OPPORTUNITY:

This was a natural work team of people from the bonding shop. All products manufactured in this business require bonding, so virtually all hardware cycles through the bond shop. The process is lengthy, and if it is done improperly the entire product must be scrapped. High throughput with a low defect rate is essential to maintain product quality and meet customer delivery schedules.

PROBLEM STATEMENT:

The team conducted a "re's" analysis on their process flow diagram. A Pareto analysis of the identified re's led them to develop three problem statements:

1. From July 19 to September 10, 41 units were manufactured. No defects were recorded during any "in-process" inspections, which verify that a "certified" manufacturing operator has performed his task as specified. These "re-checks" increase manufacturing and inspection time by an average of 1.01 hours per unit, with no added value.
2. Forty-six percent of units bonded from fiscal week FW 30 through FW 36 required rework for minor damage, such as nicks, scratches, and burrs.
3. All bonded units demonstrate overall dimensional changes from prebonded dimensions. During the period from FW 44 through FW 46, 22.4% of the units bonded recorded dimensions beyond the acceptable tolerances.

ACTION PLAN:

The team addressed the first two problems during their training sessions. By creating and analyzing the process flow diagram, they eliminated 5 of the 17 steps, including three in-process inspections. They also conducted a Pareto analysis of the locations where minor damage occurs, to gain insight into causes of the damage. (Use of the Pareto analysis is addressed in Chapter 3.) This led to several minor changes in tooling and handling devices. Efforts on the first two problem areas were progressing well, so they started work on their third problem statement. A structure tree to identify root causes was developed to investigate specific potential causes.

VERIFICATION OF RESULTS:

Changes to the assembly instructions were successfully implemented, leading to a reduction in cycle time while maintaining a high level of product quality. After changing tools and fixtures, the number of damage defects was reduced from 1.29 defects per unit to .18 defects per unit.

INSTITUTIONALIZATION PROCESS:

Work instructions have been changed and unit inspection is now used to document the location of any nicks or scratches. This is correlated with other data to help identify problem areas.

CONTINUING ACTIONS:

The team continued to review other assemblies to eliminate non-value-added steps and they tracked recurring damage defects to identify root causes. As a result of continued attention to the process, a third problem statement was developed which logically led to a root cause analysis and subsequent problem correction and prevention.

TEAM FOCUS:

Project Summary D

Quality Data Systems

AREA OF OPPORTUNITY:

This was a natural work team involved with collecting and analyzing defect and inspection data on all production hardware which in turn was reported monthly to the customer. Any adverse trends or significant problems resulted in customer audits, inspections, and deficiency reports. It was essential that the analysis be timely and accurate to help ensure customer satisfaction.

PROBLEM STATEMENT:

The team developed a process flow diagram and conducted a "re's" analysis. Initially they felt that reprocessing inaccurate data was the major problem; however, their analysis showed less than 1% of the data was inaccurate. The more pressing problem was found to be redundancy between reporting systems. This led to the problem statement:

Inspectors are duplicating efforts by inputting similar data on the Inspection Input Module Sheets and the Electronic Direct Labor Computer System.

ACTION PLAN:

A root cause analysis of why the duplication existed showed the primary reason to be the nature of the forms used. It also indicated that some inspectors required additional training to be able to complete the forms correctly. The team established a two-phase plan. The first phase focused on eliminating redundancy between the two forms, thereby saving time required by the inspectors to complete them. The second phase incorporated all the required information on the current electronic form, thereby eliminating the need for the paper form.

VERIFICATION OF RESULTS:

When phase one was completed, reporting time per inspection was reduced by approximately one minute. This resulted in a direct savings of $85 per day, or about $2,040 per month.

INSTITUTIONALIZATION PROCESS:

Data fields for the new electronic form were established for integration into the next software update. A plan for a real time data retrieval system was developed and implemented with phase two.

CONTINUING ACTIONS:

In addition to monitoring phase two of the implementation plan, the team continued to evaluate the reports generated by the system to determine if they could be reduced or eliminated.

Project Summary E

TEAM FOCUS:

Electronic Assembly Shop

AREA OF OPPORTUNITY:

This natural work team was formed in the electronic assembly area, the critical path item for production programs. The area was plagued by high scrap rates, low productivity, and schedule delays. Dramatic improvement was required to meet contract schedules.

PROBLEM STATEMENT:

The team benefited from experiences of other teams when they began analyzing their process flow diagram and were easily able to identify non-value-added steps. They also decided to focus on defects. A Pareto analysis showed damaged grommets were their worst problem. This led to the problem statement:

> During the past year, 50% of all cable defects were damaged grommets and connectors. These defects in turn resulted in rework and replacement costs near $27,000 in the shop alone (i.e., without Iceberg Effect).

ACTION PLAN:

The team analyzed the process flow diagram and eliminated non-value-added work. To reduce damaged grommet defects they developed a structure tree which identified grommet extractions as the primary cause of defects. This led to the discovery that tooling and manufacturing methods were inducing damage. Process changes to correct and prevent the damage were devised and introduced into the process.

VERIFICATION OF RESULTS:

The number of operations in the work instructions were reduced from 70 to 36 on the first cable that was studied. Since the various changes to grommet extraction procedures were implemented, the defect rate has been reduced from a high of 41% to 12%. The scrap cost has been reduced from $142 per cable to $29 per cable.

INSTITUTIONALIZATION PROCESS:

Work instructions and procedures were changed for the cable initially studied. Lessons learned were applied to all other cable harness assemblies. Training on grommet extractors was established to ensure that operators understood the new procedure and were trained to integrate the preventive actions into the daily work process.

CONTINUING ACTIONS:

The team continued to review all other assemblies in the area for similar work instruction simplifications. Since corrective action improved the grommet extraction process, they began to address the insertion process for similar improvements.

Project Summary F

TEAM FOCUS:

Final Assembly.

AREA OF OPPORTUNITY:

This was a natural work team from the manufacturing shop which performed final product assembly prior to customer review.

PROBLEM STATEMENT:

The team identified defects as the first area they wanted to address. A Pareto analysis of all defect data in the shop led to the following problem statement:

During September, the assembly package had an 89% reject rate at final inspection.

On average, there were 3.9 defects per unit. Including customer buy off, there were 5.2 defects per unit. Of all the defects, 60% were attributed to damage (nicks and scratches.) The cost of rework per reinspection and support was estimated at $10,000 during this time period.

ACTION PLAN:

A structure tree analysis helped identify manpower and methods as the main causes of damage. Analysis of the process flow diagram identified 11 unnecessary steps in the assembly sequence.

In addition several tools and fixtures were identified that could damage the units. The actions taken included (1) streamlining of assembly work instructions, (2) modification of seven tools and fixtures so that they would not damage the units, (3) clarification of work planning and inspection procedures to eliminate confusion among operators, and (4) devising methods to catalog and track recurring defects.

VERIFICATION OF RESULTS:

The number of defects per unit had been reduced from 5.2 to 1.3. The number of damage-related defects decreased from 3.7 to 1.6 per unit. The rework and reinspection costs had dropped from $10,000 per month to $3,400 per month.

INSTITUTIONALIZATION PROCESS:

Work instructions and procedures were changed and a new method for recording recurring damage-related defects was implemented. Lessons learned in this shop were applied in other shops.

CONTINUING ACTIONS:

The team followed through by working on the assembly with the next highest defect rate and conducted a similar process flow diagram analysis. The method for recording defects helped identify an area to be studied with structure tree methodology.

Team Identification

You have one last piece of work to do before you actually begin the implementation process. That is, you must clearly identify your team. You can look at this as the initial step in making meetings productive. Use your imagination when selecting a team name. You can be mundane and simply relate a team name directly to a process or product *or* you can be creative and dream up something more fun, but still appropriate. This is a good place to use your brainstorming skills. Again, remember to have fun.

Real Time Application Assignment

This marks the beginning of the implementation process where you can practice all the skills you have learned thus far. Your first assignment is not designed with skill application in mind. Rather, it will allow you to begin the process on your own and then enable you and your team to build progressively from this base. The objective is to have you begin building a list of opportunities to improve your work area. When developing your list, consider:

- Pet peeves
- Things you've learned to live with
- Things you've always wanted to do something about, but you could never get anyone to listen

After completing your personal list, keep it confidential. Later on you will share copies of this list among your team members.

2

Getting Started

In this chapter, you will be addressing four major topics:

- How do you know where to look?
- The process flow concept
- Process flow diagraming (PFD)
- What do we look for?

Once you have explored these topics and had a chance to try some new techniques, you will receive a more challenging application assignment to help internalize the CPI principles in your natural work area.

How Do You Know Where to Look?

You've each made your own personal list of what you would like to see fixed. You may have done this before just to vent some personal frustration, but you probably ripped it up and threw it away. I've gotten temporary psychological relief from doing the same thing. However, the problems kept returning to haunt me because I really never did anything about solving them or eliminating their root causes. You're probably no different. However, from this point forward you will be able to change that.

Making a personal list of things you want to see improved is a beginning. Later on when you exchange and share lists among team members, you will find a number of items in common and you may feel inclined to run right off and do something about them. Please refrain from jumping to conclusions. Just because some items are duplicated doesn't mean they are the best place to begin. Knowing where to look, knowing what you've found, and knowing exactly where and how to begin is usually a mystery. The tools and techniques of (1) brainstorming, (2) storyboarding, and (3) process flow diagraming will be used to help you solve the mystery.

You and your team were introduced to brainstorming and storyboarding in Chapter 1, and have discovered the simplicity and power of these techniques. The big questions remain:

- What do we brainstorm and/or storyboard?
- How do we figure out what, if anything on our list, we should be working on?
- What do we do first?

Process flow diagraming will help you discover where to start and what the potential "hot spots" are in your process.

Before we get into the detail of PFD, let's look at the process flow concept in some depth.

Process Flow Concept

The three main objectives we will accomplish in this section are to:

- Help you understand what constitutes a process
- Illustrate how one process can be buried within another
- Enable you clearly to define the boundaries of a process

To accomplish these objectives, we will address the following topics:

- Definitions
- What's in a process?
- The nesting concept
- How is a process controlled?

Definitions

You will recall that we extracted a definition of *process* from Webster:

A particular method of doing something, generally involving a number of steps or operations.

You will need a few additional definitions in order to understand the process flow concept. Rather than giving you Webster's definition or my interpretation, I'd like you and your team to make an initial cut at it. Define the following terms:

Input

Output

Control

Mechanism

Process boundary

Customer

Supplier

Now let's see what Webster has to say about them.

Input: The energy or power put in, as to operate a machine.

Output: 1. Production of goods, crops, work, etc. 2. The amount produced, yield.

Control: 1. Exercise power over; restrain; govern; dominate. 2. Regulate.

Mechanism: 1. Machinery. 2. The agency by which an effect is produced or a purpose accomplished.

Process boundary (this definition is offered as a combination of the two separate word definitions from Webster): The boundary line or perimeter of the steps or operations involved in a particular process.

Customer: 1. A person who buys. 2. Any person with whom one has dealings.

Supplier (this definition is offered as the my interpretation of Webster's definition of *supply*.): One who gives, furnishes or provides (what is needed or wanted).

You now have two perspectives on the terms. In the interest of consistency, I have taken the liberty to develop a set of working definitions from my perspective so you will understand how I interpret each of the terms in the pages that follow.

Input: Material or information fed into a process.

Output: Material or information that results from internal process activity.

Control: Environmental information used by the process to determine what can or should be done.

Mechanism: Resources that influence the process, i.e. people, machinery, computers, etc.

Process boundary: The limits of a particular process, sometimes defined by an imaginary box or line across which all inputs, outputs, controls, and mechanisms must be transferred.

Customer: Whoever receives the output of a process.

Supplier: Whoever provides the necessary input to a process.

What's in a Process?

It's important for us to take a closer look at what constitutes a process and its surrounding environment so you will be able to classify the various steps in a process into general categories, through the use of process flow diagramming.

Think of each step in a process as a separate entity that can be captured in a phrase on a piece of paper or a card. Next, picture a box drawn around the words. This represents the boundary of that individual step. Figure 2–1 will help you visualize my description. It also illustrates the environmental interaction of external controls and mechanisms. Finally, by adding input and output we can complete the picture.

As you might have already guessed, when the individual steps are appropriately oriented, the output from one step becomes the input to the following step. Thus the two steps that are linked together will directly influence each other. If one step is adversely affected by controls, mechanisms, or other input/output factors, the adverse conditions will have an effect on the other steps to which it is directly linked.

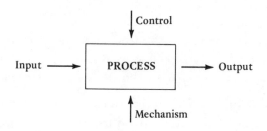

Figure 2–1

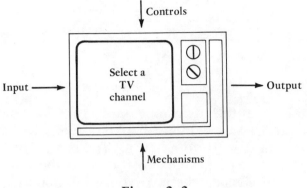

Controls

Input

Output

Mechanisms

Figure 2–2

Let's use a simple illustration to clarify any questions you may have. The object is to identify the steps in the process of selecting a TV channel.

The first step is to draw a block and identify the process inside the confines (Figure 2–2).

Next, identify the input and output. In this case, the input is the customer requirement. You are the customer and you would like to watch a specific program (see Figure 2–3). Suppose the input becomes "I want to watch Monday Night Football."

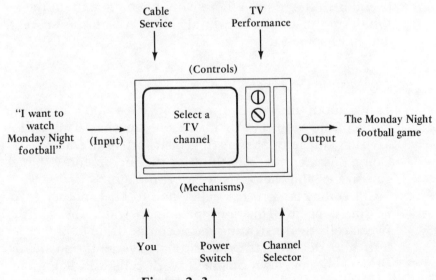

Figure 2–3

** INPUT **

"Monday Night Football"

** PROCESS **

Select the channel

Now, think about the environmental factors that control what you can watch. These are things that you usually have little control over and must learn to adapt to. The environmental input signal and the actual performance of the TV are the only governing controls we will consider here. If you think about it, I'm sure you can find more.

** CONTROLS **

Cable service, TV performance

Finally, we will limit the mechanisms that influence channel selection to you, the power switch, and the channel selector. These are definitely under your control.

** MECHANISMS **

You, power switch, channel selector

I suggest that you and your team brainstorm some additional influence factors. As a starting point, suppose your spouse or friend is in the room. Where would he or she fit on the diagram? What kind of influence would that have on the process? Try it and have some fun.

The Nesting Concept

Think about the set of measuring cups you can find in every kitchen, the type that fit inside one another. This will give you a visual image of the nesting concept we are about to discuss. Going one step further, think of the incremental change in the cup size as an echelon. Now we can begin.

CPI connects "process echelons" to one another through the nesting concept. This concept demonstrates the interaction between cells by illustrating the decomposition of higher level cells into more detailed subsets. Through segmentation and decomposition of higher level business work cells, CPI helps the natural work teams establish the relationship between their specific process and the other cells that make up the total business. As they look to higher levels, they are able to see the link to the overall mission of the business and to understand their own role in accomplishing overall business plans and goals. As they look to lower levels, they can see the impact their team's process has on those processes. An example might be the influence that a middle management team has on a lower echelon natural work team. No matter what your perspective may be, in simple terms, you can quickly assess the "contributed value" of your team.

When we address process flow diagraming (PFD) in the next section, you will discover how this actually works in a fun exercise. Meanwhile, Figure 2–4 will help illustrate how processes are nested within higher order processes. You could consider the highlighted circle in Level Zero as the single step "select a TV channel" and the Level 1 and Level 2 expansions as a detailed breakdown or microscopic view of the process.

Now that you see how to move from one level of a process to another, develop a similar model for your business.

Having developed the hierarchy of business processes to the extent that you understand where your team fits, it's time to take a closer look at your process inputs and outputs. Refer to

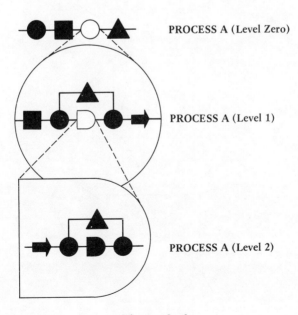

PROCESS A (Level Zero)

PROCESS A (Level 1)

PROCESS A (Level 2)

Figure 2–4

the working definitions of input and output and then think about the following questions:

1. Who supplies information, products, or services to our process?
2. Who receives the output from our process?

In effect you are asking "Who are our suppliers?" and "Who are our customers?"

The diagrams in Figure 2–5 have proven very helpful in answering these questions because they are directly adaptable to brainstorming and storyboarding.

How Is a Process Controlled?

Recalling that control can be viewed as regulating or restraining, we will now address the environmental factors that influence a

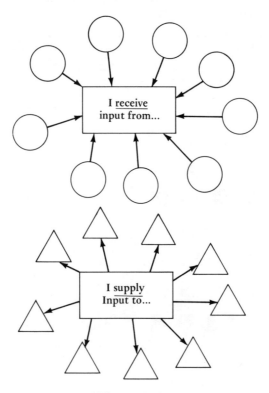

Figure 2–5

process through regulation or by causing a constraint. The factors influencing your process can occur from within that process as well as externally. I'd like you to think of the internal controls as feedback loops or mechanisms that tell you how your process is working. It's the way that your process can talk to you. All you have to do is learn how to listen. And, as we progress, you will discover ways to make that happen.

Conversely, external factors over which you have little or no control can regulate and influence your process. These are feedback indicators that let you know how well your customers are accepting the output of your process. Effective balance and integration of these two sets of controls is critical. From a business perspective, if they are not balanced and well integrated, you most probably will suffer market damage which could result in your exiting that business.

Here are two thoughts that may serve as valuable tests of your process:

- When process controls are well understood and defined, process output can be accurately predicted.
- If you cannot predict the output of your process, you probably have not identified all the controls or influence factors.

With these closing thoughts on process control, let's move on to the heart of CPI, process flow diagraming (PFD).

Process Flow Diagraming

The objectives of this section are to:

- Introduce you and your team to the powerful technique of process flow diagraming (PFD)
- Illustrate the benefits and simplicity of PFD
- Show you how it works
- Provide some basic steps for you and your team to use to apply PFD to your natural work area
- Allow you to experience PFD in action through a case study

We will accomplish these objectives by addressing the following topics:

- What is PFD?
- Why is it effective?
- What are the benefits of using PFD?
- Who is involved?
- PFD symbols.
- How does PFD really work?
- Basic steps.

Let's proceed by examining what process flow diagraming is.

What Is PFD?

Process flow diagraming is a powerful and dynamic, yet simple and effective method for graphically displaying the various steps, events, and operations that constitute any process. It provides a picture, in the form of a diagram, of what is actually happening when a product is produced for or a service is provided to a customer. It provides a firm but flexible foundation for continuous improvement by acting as a real time planning and implementation tool.

Why Is It Effective?

There is no one magical reason to explain the effectiveness of PFD. However, it appears that the power associated with a visual display of what is in your mind is one of the keys. This is based on my personal experience, experiences from CPI teams, the results reported by my colleagues, and some scientific evidence of how people think.

While discussing with a noted psychiatrist the CPI philosophy and the vast successes being experienced, I questioned him about the human thought process and shared my own impressions. I said I had figured out that I tend to think totally in pictures and thought that everyone else did the same.

Based on that hypothesis and the fact that pictures are considered to be the universal language, I made PFD the basic means of displaying personal ideas so others could see what I was thinking. My colleague informed me that there is scientific evidence to indicate that most, but not all, people think in pictures.

Therefore, supported by scientific evidence and two years of living examples generated by teams, the following explanation is offered for your use and hypothetical testing. Very simply, the visual power of PFD enables you to:

- Simplify complex processes
- Graphically document key events in your process
- Pinpoint critical areas subject to streamlining and improvement
- Paint a vivid portrait of a process rather than leaving the vague and ominous to the "assumed obvious"

Through application and broad use, many teams have proven that the graphical simplicity of PFD makes it a useful and powerful tool to help anyone understand any process. And an unexpected and welcome side effect is the enhancement of multifunctional and multilevel "natural" teamwork. Last, but certainly not least, it easily and effectively links classroom training to the everyday "working" process. This helps make it part of what you do and how you think, rather than something extra to do.

What Are the Benefits of Using PFD?

Reading the previous description of PFD, you may have begun to formulate your own opinions about its benefits. During the course of implementing the process, several CPI teams were asked to assess the value of PFD and their perceptions of its specific benefits. Here are some of their responses:

- Simplifies problem solving
- Provides a structure for thinking through a difficult process in a simplified, visible manner
- Enables you to see the entire process
- Helps magnify normally insignificant or overlooked areas and display their relevancy to problem solving and the improvement process
- Facilitates the reduction of process cycle times and work-in-process (WIP) inventory.
- Helps clearly identify nonessential and non-value-adding work so it can readily be removed from the process.
- Allows you to turn a clouded, confused situation into a logical sequence of events which can be addressed, prioritized, and analyzed in a planned and satisfying manner

- Brings focus to a team
- Enables team members to identify personal contributed value and recognize the contributions of others
- Helps the team focus on facts rather than personalities (asking *why*, not *who*).
- Enhances open, real time, supportive communication.

When PFD was introduced into a defense-related business in Florida, one team was quick to report that they had been using PFD for quite some time and proudly exhibited the diagram describing their process. But the sponsoring team manager later reported that only after "diagraming and walking the process" did they really have a true picture of it. They discovered that their original diagram had missed some important steps. Moreover, they initially thought they were doing some things that they actually weren't doing at all.

Who Is Involved?

To determine the personnel required for successfully diagraming a process, begin by identifying the members of your team, "naturally" focused on a specific process that you work with daily. Then perform the ownership test described in Chapter 1. Ad hoc members may be needed to fulfill the ownership requirements, help eliminate barriers, and act as internal customers or suppliers. The team mentioned in the previous subsection found that only after interviewing shop floor personnel were they able to accurately identify all the steps in their process. Ultimately, the shop floor people became very important ad hoc members.

As mentioned before, unless it is a cross-functional team designated to address a particular situation and then dissolve, the team, once identified, will remain intact, functional, and permanent. However, names and faces may change from time to time as personnel change job assignments. Think of this as making the process people-independent.

Management involvement and participation on the team is a fundamental requirement for several reasons. Changes in management procedures must occur in concert with process changes. Therefore, management involvement on the team can help ensure the proper changes are made to support and reinforce team activity. Once the improvement process is started, there is no turning back. To do so would be to return to "business as usual" and revert to "old habits." Measurements set by the team and management drive team activity. Therefore, they must be congruent and compatible with team and business goals.

PFD Symbols

Five of the six symbols used in PFD can be found in most industrial engineering text books.

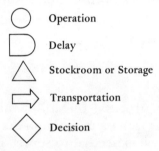

- Operation
- Delay
- Stockroom or Storage
- Transportation
- Decision

They are used to model the various steps you identify in your process. The sixth was added because it represented a way to communicate with your process.

Measurement

It is most convenient to use storyboard cards preprinted with the six symbols. Also, by using different colored cards to represent the various symbols, you can quickly identify the steps you wish to concentrate on initially. For example, should you choose red to identify delays, a glance at the completed PFD would enable you to locate these non-value-adding steps quickly. Furthermore, such a convention enables ad hoc team members to understand quickly where you want to focus your team efforts, and why.

As your diagram begins to take shape, it is important to connect the individual cards with string, yarn, or some appropriate equivalent, so the proper flow of the steps is clearly illustrated. Arrows are used to show process flow direction.

How Does PFD Really Work?

If you haven't already figured it out, PFD is best done in a storyboarding environment, and all storyboarding and brainstorming rules apply. Some teams have found it convenient or even necessary to build their diagram on a portable board. This facilitates transportation from a meeting place to the work area.

Think of your PFD as your team's foundation for continuous improvement. Once it has been fully developed it serves as the reference point for:

- Analysis
- Data collection
- Non-value-added work elimination
- Control charting
- Continuous improvement efforts

Basic Steps

Since PFD is itself a process, the following brief list of steps will guide you in developing a useful and accurate diagram. You may wish to alter steps as needed to serve your team's purposes better. However, it is recommended that they be initially followed as presented.

1. Define the process to be improved, and be certain that you clearly define the boundaries. (Don't bite off more than you can chew.)
2. Visually develop the diagram using brainstorming and story-boarding techniques.
3. Display and build the process steps using only the six basic symbols.
4. Assign a time value to each symbol.
5. Physically walk through the process to verify the accuracy of the display. Note and record missing steps.
6. Interview personnel directly involved with implementation of the process.
7. Invite your process's customers and suppliers to a presentation and walk through.
8. Change visual display to correspond with actual process steps. This is a powerful team-building tool and buy-in technique.

Remember to use all these steps, and add to them as necessary to ensure success.

What Do We Look For?

You've had the opportunity to see how PFD works and how it helps identify opportunities and areas of improvement. But how do you know if you are on the right track and whether or not you have explored enough to satisfy you and your team? It was with these thoughts in mind that the objectives of this section were created. The following topics will be addressed:

- What can be improved?
- "Re's" exercise
- Control points
- CPI opportunities

They will give you the tools to:

- Take the initial step to diagnose a process
- Learn what to look for as improvement opportunities
- Discover where to look

What Can Be Improved?

Let's begin answering this question by asking a few more. When you look at your process, is there anything obvious within the process or in the environment that causes waste? Delays? Inventory queues?

Think about your PFD card categories. What do you think you would find if you looked for the delay cards and stockroom or storage cards?

Once the obvious pulse points are spotted, it will be necessary to locate the areas within the process that are "critical to quality." At first this always leaves people kind of cold. However, as you walk through the process, remember to ask the following questions for each process step:

- Is it critical to meet customer requirements or expectations?
- Is it controlled? How?
- Does it add value to the process?

By asking these questions and by looking for delays and storage points, you will begin to uncover specific things that cause your process to supply unacceptable products or services to your customers. You will be much better able to judge what's critical and what's not. Remember, this is a judgment call from your team and, as you will learn, the CPI process has steps built in to help you verify whether or not your initial judgment was correct and help you decide what your next course of action should be.

"Re's" Exercise

The following exercise is designed to help you locate things that may have become accepted as part of the normal daily way of doing business, but should not be there. Known as the "re's" exercise, this activity will help uncover places where you may have "institutionalized failure." Let's explore this a bit further by probing with a few questions.

- Do you have places where products are sent because they have defects?
- Do certain people do nothing but fix errors?
- Is there a budget to cover corrective action for internal defects or errors?
- Is there always time for doing things over a second or third time?
- Are there things that you personally do in a normal work day that begin with the prefix "re"?

If you or your team can answer yes to any of these questions, then you have "institutionalized failure." Why? Because the message is being sent that these things are OK and acceptable.

One CPI team took on the challenge of investigating and improving the system for reviewing and dispositioning material that did not meet drawing or functional specification. This was officially known as the MRB (for Material Review Board) system. Because of the unfortunate proliferation of material that had to be dispositioned by a team of experts and the amount of time associated with the activity, the MRB system became affectionately known as "The Black Hole." MRB systems in any business are shrines to failure and indicators that it's OK not to do it right the first time because there is a system that will sort it out later. Maybe!

Now, as a team, think about all the things that you do in your business and in your specific work area that begin with the prefix "re." This exercise will help lead you in the right direction.

Once you've made your list, discuss the following questions among your team. Do not anguish over them because you will have an opportunity to take a more specific look at them in proper context to ensure you focus properly and begin your improvement process at the right place.

- Does your business have places specifically set aside for these activities?
- Do you budget for them?
- How much of your business resources do you think are wasted by not doing these things right the first time? (Remember the "Rule of Tens" and the Iceberg Phenomenon).
- Which things could you and your team do something about?
- Which one would you and your team consider as your first application project?

Answering these questions will assist you in preparing for your Real Time Application Assignment.

Control Points

A control point in a process is simply a location that can be used to regulate or monitor activity. In CPI terminology, control points are the locations where you can listen to and dialogue with your process. Before you can do so, however, you must locate the "listening points."

Where do you look for control points in a process? Probably a good place to start is with any measurement. Why? Because measurements are an indicator of what a process is doing. Also, measurements drive action and tell us how well we are doing in attaining our goals. Think about the measurement symbol you were introduced to on page 71. Once you located those cards in your process, wouldn't you have identified the control points where you can begin a dialogue?

When you have identified the measurement cards, you must decide if they represent the correct listening points. Once that is determined, you can effectively listen to and interpret your process. But for now, you need to know if you have the right points.

Remember, you are a "process-focused" team. Therefore, you must focus on the indicators that will ensure effective management of your process so that your customers will be satisfied with the products and services that emerge at the end. Therefore, the measurements or process control points you select must:

- Provide the right data
- Support process improvement
- Drive process management
- Enable you to listen to and dialogue with your process

CPI Opportunities

You will recall that the Real Time Application Assignment in Chapter 1 asked you to list those things that you would personally like to see changed. You were also asked to make copies for your team members but to hold them until the proper time. Distribute copies of personal lists among team members. The composite list which results from combining all inputs represents your team's CPI opportunity list. This list will be factored in to defining what's critical in Chapter 3.

The Real Time Application Assignment you are about to address will help put all these things in perspective. It is designed to help you and your team figure out what your process looks like and how to go about streamlining and improving it.

Real Time Application Assignment

The objectives of this assignment are clear and simple:

- Facilitate practical application of newly learned skills on the job.
- Have your team develop a process flow diagram for your "natural" work area.
- Further develop your list of opportunities for improvement.
- Help you locate specific areas to be improved in your work area.

Using the tools and techniques learned in this chapter:

1. Diagram your process using cards and PFD symbols.
2. Record your PFD on a worksheet.

3. "Walk" the process to verify accuracy.
4. Note missing steps.
5. Invite customers and suppliers to walk through the process.
6. Test the steps for:
   • criticality
   • necessity
   • value
7. Perform a "re's" analysis and record locations on the PFD.

Practice on the Job

Most teams recognize on-the-job application as a critical point in CPI because it is here that they begin to work together as a real team. As you proceed with the steps described in this assignment and others to follow, you will discover that barriers will be eliminated and some "sacred cows" will disappear from the scene. This won't happen by magic—but you will find that the things you once could only talk about as individuals will be possible as a team.

3

What's Critical?

Now that you've completed Chapters 1 and 2, you and your team have discovered how CPI can help you and how to get started with the process. You've also completed two application assignments which should have helped reinforce the applied value of the tools and techniques learned thus far.

This chapter deals with deciding what's critical in your implementation process. To help you determine this, you will be introduced to three new topics:

- Deciding what to do first
- Stating the problem
- Analyzing the problem

I suggest that you take time to share applications and experiences with other teams to help reinforce the process and assist cross-functional integration. The first section in this chapter will serve as a guideline for decision making. Other teams have found this activity particularly helpful in building trust and reinforcing teamwork.

Deciding What to Do First

The objectives of this section are:

- To take an in-depth look at Pareto analysis and the Nine Block
- To investigate the effects of real-world cost drivers
- To help you prioritize opportunities for improving your process

After we explore these topics, you will have the opportunity to complete an exercise to help internalize the concepts.

Pareto Analysis

Deciding what to do first can be difficult and sometimes overwhelming. The most important thing is oftentimes not the most obvious. You may find yourselves being continuously reactive because without constant attention to the big picture, you tend to jump from one thing to another and forget about what you may have just fixed. When that happens, well-intended corrective action without proper follow-through usually results in deterioration and eventual recurrence of the problem. What would be most helpful would be a judgmental tool that would help identify what to work on first and then indicate a logical sequence of corrective and preventive actions.

Pareto analysis provides you with a simple and effective method of:

- Focusing on what to do first
- Identifying what will yield the most benefit for the least effort
- Keeping track of what to do next
- Continuously focusing on improvement

To paraphrase the Pareto principle, which was invented by an Italian statistician of the same name:

80% of the problem is often caused by only 20% of the contributors

Conversely, if we attend to the correct 20%, we can fix 80% of the problem. That's nice, but who is smart enough to know how to find the 20%? How do we focus on the "critical few" rather than the "trivial many"? By working through a few simple examples you will discover exactly how to make that happen with a high level of confidence.

Stated in terms more familiar to you, the Pareto principle might look like this:

- 20% of the customers will account for 80% of sales. (It's marketing's job to find the critical 20%.)
- 20% of the process problems can be traced to 80% of the scrap and rework. (Look out! There's a "re.")

- 20% of your opportunity list (see CPI opportunities, Chapter 2) list will yield most of the benefits to your process. (Look for the top 20!)

Ultimately you can use the Pareto principle to narrow down your list so you can truly get the most by focusing on the least. Don't get the idea that you are getting something for nothing because you're not. Remember, there is "no free lunch." You will have to work with your team to find the 20%, but it will be worth the effort. A Pareto analysis is presented below to illustrate the principle and demonstrate the power and simplicity of the tool.

EXAMPLE

DEFCON, the defense-based business referred to in Chapter 1, identified seven areas where defects were interrupting the production cycle.

Electronics	46%
Pre-assembly	24%
Harness	9%
Final assembly	8%
Machine	7%
Transponder	4%
Plate, alodine	2%

Since the electronics shop accounted for almost half of the reported problems, a CPI team decided to analyze the defects found in that particular area. Eight defect categories were identified.

Damage	43%
Electrical assembly	20%
Termination	11%
Planning	8%
Defective parts	6%
Identification	5%
Potting/bonding	4%
Drawing/spec	3%

Damage accounted for 43% of all electronics shop defects and 20% of all problems (46% of 43% = 20%). Based on these observations the team decided to focus their efforts on damaged parts in the electronics shop. You may have intuitively concluded the same thing. However, the analysis supports the intuition and helps remove doubt.

Suppose you were not as fortunate as this team and found yourself faced with analyzing defect information gathered over a period of five months. The data has been logged in tabular form as shown below and you need to determine quickly what happened in February and explain your findings to a large diverse group of operators and managers.

Organization	*% Defects*				
	Jan	*Feb*	*Mar*	*Apr*	*May*
Engineering	12	14	10	13	13
Harness area	8	5	6	7	5
Electronics shop	30	35	28	32	35
Machine/sheet metal shop	15	10	12	12	14
Planning	1	2	1	3	1
Vendor/subcontractor	6	6	5	4	5
Preassembly shop	18	20	26	21	24
Inspection	10	8	12	8	3
Total	100	100	100	100	100

Is it easy to decipher and could you easily explain what happened, including identification of the biggest hitters? The answer is obviously no, but what could you do to simplify and clarify your situation?

Let's begin by extracting the February information from the table and plotting it on a bar chart (Figure 3–1).

Now, that's a lot better. But, don't stop yet. All we have done is simply transferred the chart data to a graph. You still need to identify the big hitters. While you're at it, why don't you show your audience how defects from all the organizations lined up?

By rank ordering the data in bar chart form you have created a Pareto chart (Figure 3–2). Compare this to the complex tabular format. Your presentation has just taken on an entirely new twist. Ordering the data in this way makes it very easy to:

- Identify the big hitters
- Rank the defect rates by operation
- Quickly identify the "critical few"

The Cost Driver

Before leaving the topic of the Pareto principle, you must be aware of another very important consideration. Do not overlook the costs associated with defects and their impact on the customer. Once a Pareto analysis has been performed using defect volume or a similar parameter, you should perform a second Pareto analysis based on cost. Let's take another look at the table of defect data. However, this time let's see what the rank ordering of defect costs tells you (see Figure 3–3).

Now you have another serious contender as a focal point. Vendor defects cost you almost $35,000 during the month while the

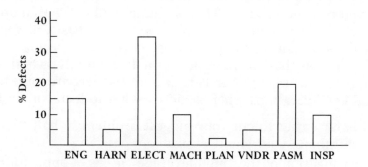

Figure 3–1. *Product Defects by Responsibility*

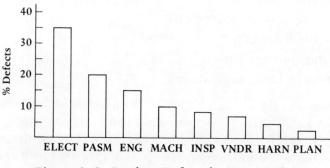

Figure 3–2. *Product Defects by Responsibility*

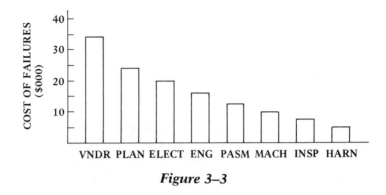

Figure 3–3

electrical shop defects cost you $20,000. The question you now face is a very pragmatic one. Do you focus on the high electrical shop defect rate or the high vendor costs? You might even consider the "double whammy" you get from the electrical shop in high defect rate coupled with relatively high defect cost.

You may be able to do more about the electrical shop situation than you can the vendors. This is a judgment call based on your business environment, and there may be no best answer. The call will be tough, but it will be easier and can be much more intelligent now that you have performed your analysis both ways.

Before closing the topic on Pareto analysis there are some fundamental considerations when deciding what to focus on first:

- It is far easier to cut your biggest problem in half than it is to eliminate your smallest problem entirely.
- Identification of the "high leverage" areas of opportunity directs attention and resources to where improvement would provide the greatest benefit.
- Time and money are *always limited*, therefore, seek
  - The greatest improvement
  - For the least effort
  - In the shortest time
  - With the least expenditure

In summary, Pareto analysis should always be based on hard data and your intuitive observations. However, you should always refocus yourself by performing a second analysis while considering cost. This is critical because the cost of process failures directly affects the bottom line. And you must ensure you are paying attention to the areas that will reap the greatest benefits. One major caution: *Don't ever let cost override customer satisfaction.* Think of the two analyses as parallel activities which should always be performed in concert with each other.

Wisely used, Pareto analysis will help you identify:

- Where the major problem lies
- Where to focus effort and resources to make the greatest impact
- Where you can have the greatest impact for the least cost

This will tell you what to do first. Once you have successfully addressed the first problem area, your Pareto tool will provide you with a logical place to begin looking for what to do next!

EXERCISE

Gather data from an area of your business that is of concern to your team and apply the Pareto technique.

Nine Block

The objective of this topic is to introduce you to another important judgmental tool, called the Nine Block. The name comes from the square divided into nine segments shown in Figure 3–4.

You will notice that the vertical side of the blocks are labeled

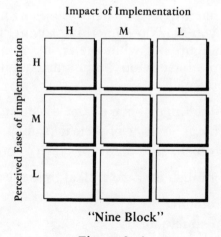

"Nine Block"

Figure 3–4

"perceived ease of implementation," with H, M, and L attached to the three separate blocks. The horizontal blocks are labeled "impact" of implementation, again with H, M, and L appropriately affixed to denote high, medium, and low. Let's briefly explore how to use this tool.

Suppose you consider your initial itemized list of the things you wanted to change, and suppose you have very little, if any, data to support your feelings. You could simply look at each item and make a judgment about whether changing it would have high, medium, or low impact on the business or your work area. Also, you could classify each item according to the ease with which you and your team could do something about correcting it. Once these two judgment calls are made, you simply draw a Nine Block and insert the numbers assigned to each item in the appropriate box, i.e., those with high impact that are easy to accomplish go in the upper left-hand box marked H and H. Follow the same convention until you have exhausted your list and placed all items in the appropriate boxes.

What do you work on first? Anything that fell in the H-H box should be considered as a starting point. The one you decide to begin with can be determined by reaching a team consensus. As you learned earlier, if no consensus can be reached, you can resort to multivoting.

Stating the Problem

Once you have narrowed your field of opportunities to the few that you know you can do something about, the next step in the process is to figure out what the problem is. This may seem ridiculously simple and obvious at the start, but it isn't necessarily so. You will need to:

- Understand the importance of clearly stating a problem
- Define the characteristics of a clear problem statement
- Analyze a problem statement for clarity and accuracy

To help you accomplish this, we will address the following topics:

- What is a problem?
- The problem statement

This will be followed by an exercise to help reinforce the basics of these tools.

What Is a Problem?

Webster defines a *problem* as:

A difficult or perplexing matter; a proposition to be worked out.

From a process orientation, a problem is:

Anything that could cause your process to provide a product or service that would fail to meet customer needs or expectations.

In any case, before you can solve a problem the first thing to do is clearly identify what it is.

All too often problems are vague and ill defined because people tend to talk about them in qualitative terms. You need to know exactly what's wrong before you set out to fix it. Unless you and your team can accurately identify and agree upon the real problem, you may end up treating the symptom instead of correcting the problem and preventing it from recurring.

The Problem Statement

A problem statement is simply a clear expression of what the problem is so it can be easily understood and articulated by any and all team members.

The two examples below illustrate correct and incorrect problem statements.

INCORRECT: Engineering change notices have increased 32% in the first quarter because the engineering department was reorganized in January.

CORRECT: Engineering change notices have increased 32% in the first quarter.

The first statement is tainted with judgment; the second simply states a fact based on verifiable and quantifiable data. A statement that expresses the problem in specific terms is indispensable in the problem-solving process. Let's look at a hypothetical situation.

Suppose your manager or supervisor says to you: "Our scrap rate is absolutely ridiculous. You'd better get your arms around the situation before all hell breaks loose."

You heard it, but what do you do about it? After you've probed the issue a bit further, you can better describe the situation: "The scrap rate in the machine shop is 12% higher than it was last month."

Now you have something you can address and do something about. Why? Because, now you know:

- Where the situation is occurring
- How much it changed
- The time span under consideration

Development of a clear, precise statement helps you:

- Confirm that a problem actually exists
- Begin the resolution process
- Focus on "what" rather than "who"
- Clearly state the situation to others who may need to be resources to resolve the situation.

EXERCISE

Select a project your team has worked on, or consider something from your opportunity list, and prepare a clear problem statement describing the situation.

Analyzing the Problem

Now that you can recognize a good problem statement and understand the basic elements well enough to write one on your own, it's time to examine some simple, logical steps you can use to analyze a problem. Some of this may be new to you and some of it may be very familiar. In either case, take the time to follow along closely and attentively. Because, like process flow diagraming, these analytical steps need to be methodically applied to ensure that you systematically and effectively address your problem.

Let's begin by familiarizing you with some simple tools and techniques to assist in analyzing and prioritizing problems so you can logically address the root cause.

Cause and Effect Analysis

Cause and effect analysis is a judgmental technique used to link a problem to its possible causes in a systematic fashion. Having such a tool is very important when you encounter a problem that cannot be analyzed by collecting and studying numerical data. If you don't have a systematic way to approach a nonnumerical situation, then your results will be left to chance, leading ultimately to uncertainty and frustration.

Cause and effect analysis enables you to:

- Organize the problem-solving process
- Use what you know about the problem
- Logically address possible causes
- Work systematically from what you know to what you don't know
- Efficiently and logically utilize the expertise of people who have first-hand knowledge of the problem or associated process

Let's turn our attention to the graphical representation of cause and effect analysis known as a structure tree.

Structure Tree

You can readily see why the diagram in Figure 3–5 is called a structure tree. The simple link between the problem or the effect and its possible causes is represented by a straight line. If you rotate the page clockwise you will find the causes at the base of the tree forming the "root structure." Hence, the term "root cause."

The 5Ms

The structure tree diagram in Figure 3–5 has five roots connected to the problem statement block. This didn't happen by chance.

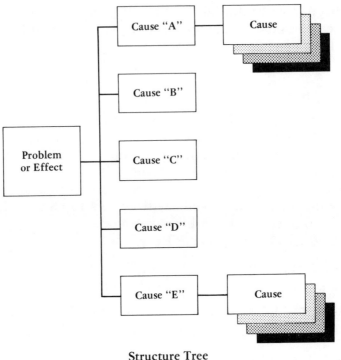

Structure Tree

Figure 3–5

All probable root causes can be classified into five categories. These are sometimes referred to as the "five Ms" and for our purposes they are identified as follows:

- Materials
- Machines
- Manpower
- Methods
- Measurements

As probable causes are identified, you assign a percentage of the potential contributed value of each one to the total problem. The total contribution must add up to 100%. To better understand how the structure tree works, let's walk through some simple steps used to construct a sample tree. Notice that the structure trees that follow are devoid of connecting lines. However, the focal points are boxed to give you a view of what it might look like in storyboard form.

Developing a Structure Tree

The following seven steps should be used in constructing any structure tree. No steps should be skipped. It's important to follow the simple logic to help get you in the habit of methodically constructing each step and avoid jumping to conclusions.

1. Prepare a problem statement or a paraphrased representation and record it on a storyboard card. If you don't have immediate access to cards, improvise.
2. Construct the "roots" and add the 5Ms
   - Materials
   - Manpower
   - Measurements
   - Machines
   - Methods
3. Assign a percentage to each M based on your judgment of contributed value to causing the problem. Remember that they must total 100%. Figure 3–6 shows what the tree might look like at this point.
4. Now locate the highest contributing factor and list the possible causes for that M.
5. Next assign percentages to the possible causes for the highest M. Here it is important to note that the total must add up to the percentage you assigned to the M. For example, if the M accounts for 80%, the total of the potential causes must add up to 80% (see Figure 3–7).
6. Develop additional levels as necessary to reach the "root cause" level. A good rule of thumb is to ask yourself "Why?"

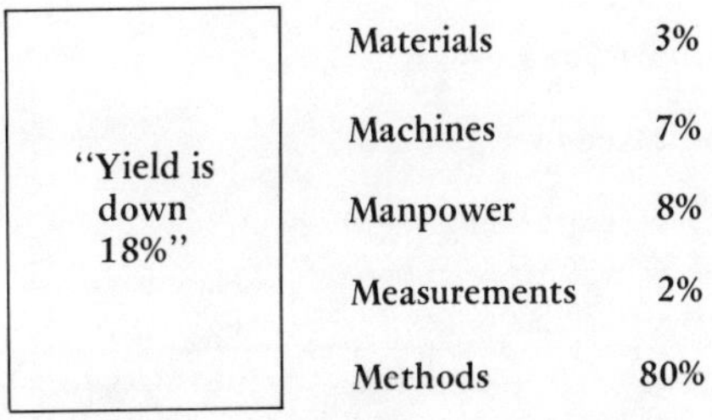

	Materials	3%
	Machines	7%
"Yield is down 18%"	Manpower	8%
	Measurements	2%
	Methods	80%

5 M's

Figure 3–6

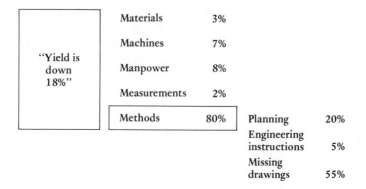

Figure 3–7

at least five times to help guide you to the root cause and avoid jumping to conclusions (see Figure 3–8).

7. As a final step, identify the corrective and preventive action required to eliminate the root cause for you and for those who will follow you.

Structure Tree Rules

Since several of the rules you have already learned apply to this process, it is important to take a moment and recap what they are. It will probably not come as a surprise that they are a combination of the Ground Rules originally introduced in Chapter 1 and the rules for brainstorming and storyboarding.

1. Brainstorm the process with a team of five to seven people who "own" the process area.

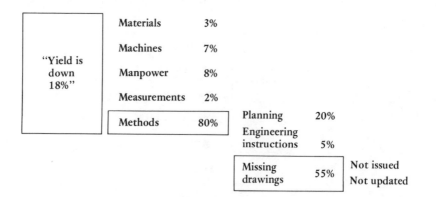

Figure 3–8

2. Select a leader to keep you on track and facilitate the process. (If the leader tries to dominate the process, however, it won't work.)
3. Identify a writer or recorder.
4. Develop your structure tree in a storyboard environment. Follow the rules applicable to storyboarding and use the tools.
5. Generate as many ideas as possible using the 5Ms as category headings.
6. Avoid early discussion of any idea.
7. Keep the process moving.
8. Totally avoid criticism of all ideas.
9. "Hitchhike" on the ideas of others.
10. Invite "experts" as ad hoc members to assist in the process. This is critical to total ownership.

Do's and don'ts

Use the following tips in conjunction with the previous list of rules. They were compiled from notes gathered in actual implementation sessions.

1. Don't get obsessed with neatness during the construction process. It's better to let the ideas flow freely. The final tree can be cleaned up for record purposes.
2. If you are doubtful about the analysis or your direction, stop and refer to the problem statement before proceeding.
3. Rewrite or restate the problem statement to focus your efforts.
4. Examine the assigned percentages and reassign values as necessary.
5. Encourage thinking beyond the typical horizons. It is the responsibility of the leader to encourage and guide this process.
6. Call "time-outs" as necessary to prevent burnout or to gather data.
7. Remember, the objective is to get to the root cause. Don't jump to conclusions or attempt band-aid solutions.
8. Ask "Why?" at least five times to assist in getting to the root cause.

9. Verify root cause, identify action required to eliminate it, implement action, and verify corrective action by appropriate testing.
10. When corrective and preventive action has been established it is time to *plan, act, verify,* and then *institutionalize.*

Ishikawa Diagram

The Ishikawa diagram is yet another variation of the structure tree. Its construction has given it its nickname, the "fishbone" diagram. Construction follows the same rules as the structure tree. However, Ishikawa diagrams typically don't apply percentages to the 5Ms and thus lack the numerical judgment link. Some people choose to use a variation of both and construct an Ishikawa diagram with percentages.

The first diagram in Figure 3–9 illustrates initial construction of an Ishikawa diagram; the second demonstrates utilization.

Structure Tree vs. Ishikawa Diagram

As you might guess, the choice of one diagram over the other is strictly personal. As mentioned in the previous discussion, you can use personal variations to reach your final destination—the root cause of the problem. To aid in selection, the following comparative comments are included for your consideration:

- The purpose of both diagrams is essentially the same.
- The Ishikawa diagram typically does not use percent probability of cause.
- The structure tree is more easily expandable into additional root systems when "asking why five times."
- Both diagrams are effective in relating problems to probable causes

Whichever diagram you and your team choose, the most important realization at this point is the innate power of the visual diagram. Any visual technique you can employ will help to clarify the problem and assist you and your team in arriving at a logical consensus on the root cause and subsequent corrective action.

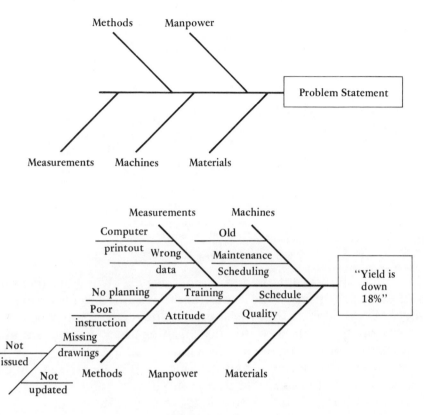

Figure 3–9

EXERCISE

Brainstorm a complaint you might hear in the office relative to room temperature. Then write a clear problem statement and construct an appropriate structure tree or Ishikawa diagram.

Frequency Charts

The general manager of an appliance distribution company was receiving complaints from customers about late shipments. Records to track shipments had always been kept in a log book which was securely locked in the file cabinet of the shipping department manager. The general manager and the shipping department manager reviewed the log book data and found it to

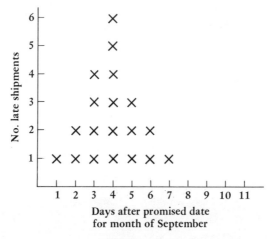

Figure 3–10

be outdated, incomplete, and almost useless. Knowing they had to get to the bottom of the situation they decided to try an experiment. They decided that the shipping supervisor would post two charts on the wall next to the shipping dock to log shipping information as it occurred. The charts (Figures 3–10 and 3–11) were examined at the end of a month. Let's see what they can tell us and the managers of that company.

By examining Figure 3–10 you can immediately see:

- The latest shipment was seven days past due
- The number of shipments missed for the month was 19.

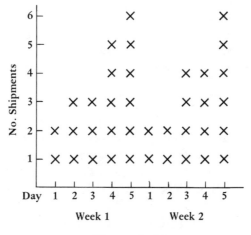

Figure 3–11

What else can you learn from this picture?

• The greatest number of shipments missed on any one day was six.

• Lateness of shipments ranged from one to seven days.

• The most shipments missed on any one day occurred four days after the promise date.

As you can readily see, a frequency chart displays data visually and a quick glance at it will tell you much more than information buried in a log book ever could.

When we look at the second chart (Figure 3–11), it is immediately obvious that the cycle of shipments increases toward the end of each week. With some imagination, some conclusions and connections can probably be made between the late shipments and the obvious weekly cycle.

Think about the value of these charts to the management team and the workers compared to a log book buried in a file cabinet. A further example should reinforce the value of frequency charts.

A large manufacturer of rotating equipment learned that their equipment was developing vibration problems during operation. During the initial steps of their investigation the manager of manufacturing found that some of the assemblers had been collecting and plotting bolt tightening data from quality data sheets. Some of the operators had discovered that it was easier and more useful to display the information on a chart rather than to let it sit idle and unused in the data sheets.

The first chart they compiled is shown in Figure 3–12. A cursory

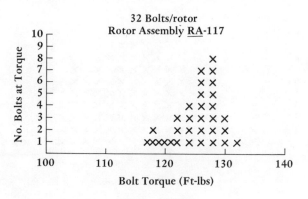

Figure 3–12

glance told them that the 32 bolts holding rotor assembly RA-117 together:

- Were tightened with a particular torque
- Had torque values ranging from 117 ft-lbs to 132 ft-lbs

A little further investigation showed:

- The torques were clustered together.
- The center of the cluster fell between 128 and 130 ft-lbs.
- There are no values that appear to be "out of whack."

This graphic display allowed the operators to see immediately what was going on in the assembly process rather than trying to construct a picture from a log book.

Next, having discovered the visual power of the frequency chart for the one rotor, they decided to resurrect data from the log sheets covering the rotors built over the time period the rotor vibration was occurring. The chart in Figure 3–13 illustrates their findings.

By building and studying this new chart they discovered:

- It was tedious plotting all the data points.
- The display became very busy and difficult to decipher.

Since they were focusing on a band of torque values defined in the engineering design specs, they decided to turn the frequency chart into a *frequency bar chart* by bracketing bands of values.

So the chart with all the data points was *simplified* as follows:

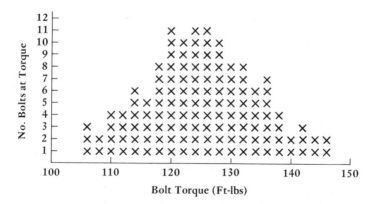

Figure 3–13

- Torque value intervals were bracketed around the design range of 120 ft-lbs to 124 ft-lbs.
- A bracket interval of 4 ft-lbs was established to cluster data.
- All values within a particular range were added together.
- The total in each bracket was plotted.

The result is illustrated in Figure 3–14. This new chart made it easy to see how many torque values fell within the "spec" limits and how many fell outside, especially on the low side.

Judicious selection of band width is necessary to ensure you do not lose sight of the objective. In this example, it was important to select a band width comparable to the spec value. If the interval had been selected without the spec limits in mind and the width had been much greater, the result could have looked like Figure 3–15 and yielded much less information.

It was determined that bolts with torque values equal to or greater than the spec limits would not contribute to the vibration problem. Therefore the chart would help segment the good from the bad but would tell little else.

As a rule of thumb, you won't go too far astray if you use six to twelve bands or intervals. The case of three as shown in Figure 3–15 limited the analysis and most probably would have led to

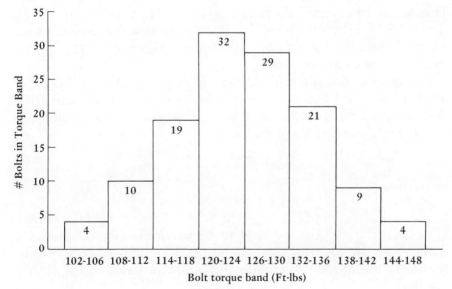

Figure 3–14

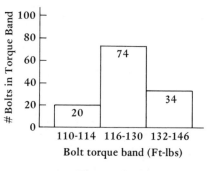

Figure 3–15

erroneous interpretation. In our case, eight intervals was satisfactory.

FREQUENCY CHART EXERCISE

Discuss an area specific to your natural team and identify an opportunity where you could apply a frequency chart. Collect the necessary data and create a frequency chart.

Defect Concentration Diagrams

We will now look at one last tool to assist in analyzing a problem. This is not to say that there are no more. However, in line with the K.I.S.S. principle (keeping it straightforward and simple), we will limit the tools to be introduced to a minimum required to add value to the process.

The defect concentration diagram is yet another visual tool used to pinpoint defects in a product or process. By directing you to the problem areas, this type of diagram can lead to identification and elimination of root causes.

SITUATION

In the manufacture of television picture tubes, a part of the assembly called the mask was found to be particularly susceptible to damage in the form of dents. The mask, which is very fragile, requires handling during inspection and transfer into the assembly line.

To help locate the defects and identify the root cause, defect

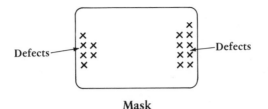

Mask

Figure 3–16

concentration diagrams were placed at the inspection work stations to record the defects as they were identified. Figure 3–16 illustrates how this was done by marking the defect with an "X."

From the charts it was immediately obvious that the defects were occurring near the edges. Further investigation led to the root cause: improper handling of the mask by untrained personnel. Once the situation was identified, the charts were used to illustrate the problem and its specific location. Operators began to pay attention to proper handling and the dent defects began to disappear.

SITUATION

An electronics business found that surface flatness and module perpendicularity defects accounted for 35% of all hardware rejects. Drawing tolerances were very tight with essentially no margin for error. Existing inspection techniques and data were useless in solving the problem.

A defect concentration diagram was designed to map the surface of the mounting pad. Each time a defect was detected it was located on the chart with an "X" (Figure 3–17). By mapping the defects as shown, it was soon noticed that the majority were occurring within two areas while the rest of the mounting surface was within tolerance. Further investigation showed that two different tools were used to machine the top portion of the pad. One of the tools was found to be the source of the problem.

As you can see, defect concentration diagrams are simple, flexible, and powerful. If you use a bit of imagination and common

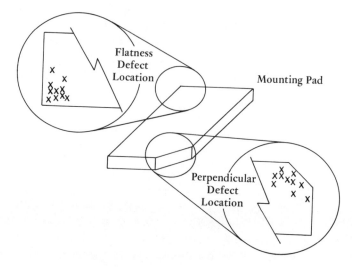

Figure 3–17

sense they can be put to invaluable use because they help to paint a picture of what's happening and where.

There are additional tools to assist in the analytical process, such as scatter diagrams and multi-vari charts. However, we will not touch on them here. Investigation and utilization of those or any additional techniques is left to you and your team.

DEFECT CONCENTRATION DIAGRAM EXERCISE

Brainstorm how and where in your natural work area you might apply a defect concentration diagram. Don't overlook opportunities such as forms with missing information.

Real Time Application Assignment

Using the accumulated tools and techniques presented in Chapters 1 and 2, along with previous application experience, implement the newly learned techniques from this chapter. The following steps are included as a general guide.

1. Review and prioritize your "re's" list.
2. Prepare a problem statement for the highest priority "re."

3. Identify key process variables for the problem statement and analyze them using the structure tree or Ishikawa method.
4. Identify possible root causes.
5. Collect data associated with the problem that provides history and activity for at least one month.

4

Listening to Your Process

Completion of Chapter 3 and the Real Time Application Assignment has given you an opportunity to put into practice the tools and techniques introduced thus far, and to experience their real value. However, up to this point communication with your process has only been one way.

As you well know from human relations, one-way communication is relatively useless and ineffective. Open dialogue is essential to ensure you and those with whom you wish to communicate are heard and are able to voice opinions openly without others criticizing or jumping to conclusions. One-way communication allows you to operate on your judgment alone. Judgment leads to assumptions and unfounded assumptions usually lead to faulty results.

In human relations, dialogue allows you to test your judgment. Open dialogue requires effective, active listening. The same is true for communication with a process. Operating with a set of preconceived ideas or judgments is a natural starting point but unless you are able to listen to your process, you will never be able to test your judgments for validity or learn anything from the process.

The objective of this chapter is to help you begin the dialoguing process by learning how to listen to your process. To accomplish this, you will be introduced to or reacquainted with the concepts of:

- Process performance
- Process capability
- Specifications vs. process capability
- Variability

- Variability and control
- Control charts
- Control limits
- Practical use of control charts

Process Performance

In this section we will explore the idea of communicating with a process in order to:

- Help you effectively screen and utilize data
- Understand what you can learn from your process

With those objectives in mind, we will explore the following topics:

- How can your process talk to you?
- Defining data
- Collecting data from a PFD
- Evaluating data
- What can the data tell us?

How Can Your Process Talk to You?

At first the concept of a process talking to you may seem strange. However, it really is not. Furthermore, if you consider what you have learned thus far about your process and the experience you've gained from application of some simple tools and techniques, you have everything necessary to listen effectively to your process. Let's proceed and develop the concept.

There is much more to a process than input and output. Unfortunately, many of us tend to look at the business process with that narrow approach, and with little or no regard for the environmental drivers. As you learned by developing your process flow diagram (PFD), a process consists of many steps, work stations, and actions. The sum total of the steps represents the means by which you and your team attempt to fulfill the expectations of your customers and, as you learned in earlier chapters, certain steps or characteristics are critical to delivering a product or service suitable to your customer. Recognizing and measuring these critical characteristics are the keys to:

- Understanding what's happening in a process
- Operating consistently at full capacity

Determining whether or not process steps "add value" is also a means of streamlining that process to ensure that such variables as cycle time, turn times, cost, and schedule can be measured and improved upon.

If you are still wondering how a process can talk to you, it's time to look at the data that can be collected, analyzed, interpreted, and used to your advantage.

Defining Data

What is data? To be grammatically correct, the question must be "What are data?" because data is the plural of the Latin word *datum.*

Data are nothing more than bits of information gathered to help understand and analyze the characteristics of a process. In the vernacular, data may be referred to as "info," statistics, or output, and the word "data" itself is often treated as a singular noun form, as it will be here.

According to Webster's *New World Dictionary,* data are defined as:

Things known or assumed; facts or figures from which conclusions can be inferred; information.

Realistically, you can think of data as:

The language of a process.

EXERCISE

With that concept in mind, you and your team should brainstorm a list of data or "words" you can obtain from your process.

Collecting Data from a PFD

Where do you find data? How do you know where to look and what to look for? To help answer these questions, refer to your PFD and identify the measurement symbols. Then record what information is being collected and where.

Also, identify and list additional data and collection points which, in the judgment of your team, may be necessary for your process to meet the requirements and expectations of your customer.

Evaluating Data

Now that you have identified the data that is being collected, where it comes from, what additional information you might need, and where you can get it, it is very important to establish the intrinsic value of each piece of data. Simply stated, you must be able to determine whether or not data collected from your process:

- Assists in problem solving
- Supports problem prevention
- Helps control the process
- Is critical to process improvement
- Supports process management
- Helps ensure customer satisfaction

EXERCISE

As a team, brainstorm and record questions you might ask to determine whether or not your process data has value. The list you compile will help you as you perform the next application assignment.

To make your list as complete as possible and to screen your process data as effectively as possible, consider expanding your list with some of the following questions compiled from team experience:

- Does it help control the process? How?
- Does it help interpret process activity? How?
- How is the information collected?
- Why is it important?
- Is it used immediately?
- Is it stored? Why and where?
- Where is it used and why?
- Is it ever used after being stored? If not, why collect it?
- When is it used and how?
- Who uses it? Why and how?

Once you have developed a list of questions to the satisfaction of your team, it should be typed and distributed to each team member for reference and posted next to your PFD. Now your team has a means of evaluating and screening process data. In addition, you have expanded and recorded the language used to dialogue with your process.

Remember, if you simply collect data and store it in a book, file, or computer, chances are you will never see it again, let alone use it. In the worst case, you may be creating a problem for some poor unsuspecting person in the future who may be assigned the fruitless and time-wasting task of trying to figure out why it was ever collected and if it has any value. Therefore, it is very important that you develop and use your information screen to clearly define:

- What you collect
- How it will be used
- Where it will be used
- When it will be used
- Whether or not it will be stored
- If stored, where and for how long
- Why will it be used
- Who will use it

Then, and only then, will you and your team be prepared to listen effectively to your process and to understand what it can tell you.

What Can the Data Tell Us?

Gathering information is just the beginning of the interpretation process. Using it in a logical, scientific manner can help you recognize trends, shifts, and deviations from expected performance. These might indicate possible problems that can be prevented before they occur. On a positive note, you can also recognize consistent performance and use that to your advantage to control and continuously improve the process.

Recalling the process flow concept discussed in Chapter 2, feedback loops within the process and from environmental sources help you to dialogue with your process. Proper utilization of these feedback mechanisms is essential where you rely heavily on people to make the process work because they allow dialogue between the people and the process. They are points of communication which enable you and your team to:

• Understand the process
• Focus on process activity rather than process output
• Predict process output performance
• Keep a finger on the process "pulse"

Focusing on process activity vs. output is critical. For example, in low-volume manufacturing processes, different products and services may be produced at one station. Therefore, attention to the repetitive critical steps at that work station should be the focal point because they may have significant impact on the output quality of the process.

In nonmanufacturing processes such as those found in service type industries, focusing on the process is even more critical. Why? Because if the process steps are not well defined, clearly explained, and totally understood, the process becomes very "people dependent." When that occurs, you have a high probability that process output cannot be accurately predicted which leads to process variation. And, that's exactly what you want to avoid.

To illustrate the consequences of people-dependent processes, take a few moments to think about the processes you use that could give you unpredictable results. Next, relate the capability of those processes to customer satisfaction.

Process Capability

A clear understanding of process capability is necessary before we proceed further. Therefore, the objectives of this section are:

• To develop a working definition of process capability
• To recognize and understand the simplicity and importance of scientific discipline

Let's begin by looking at some definitions.

Definitions

By combining definitions of its individual components, we can build a definition of *process capability*.

Recalling Webster's definition of *process* from Chapter 1:

A particular method of doing something, generally involving a number of steps or operations.

Webster also defines *capability* as:

the quality of being capable; practical ability.

Process capability can thus be defined as:

The natural or normal behavior of a process after the unnatural or abnormal disturbances affecting the process have been eliminated.

Process capability *indices* are:

Numerical measurements of the ability of a process to maintain specification limits. The most commonly used are the Cp and Cpk indices. For a more detailed discussion, it is recommended that you refer to a statistical process control handbook or text.

Now that we have a working definition for these four items, let's take a look at an example to get a better feel of how they apply to real life.

Example

A punch press operation is used to produce parts for a small appliance manufacturer. A critical dimension of a toaster base is 5.500 ± 0.004 inches. Samples from the manufacturing process were selected at random and measured by the quality control personnel. The results were plotted as shown in Figure 4–1.

It is readily apparent that a number of parts did not meet the specification limits and were unfit for use. Also, it was noticed that the process spread, the difference between the largest measured value and the smallest value, was greater than the allowed spread calculated from the specification limits.

process spread: 5.509–5.495 = 0.014

specification spread: 5.504–5.496 = 0.008 in.

The shape of the curve obtained by plotting the data shows there is a problem. The data does not form the classic bell-shaped curve expected from a "normal" process. Process analysis showed:

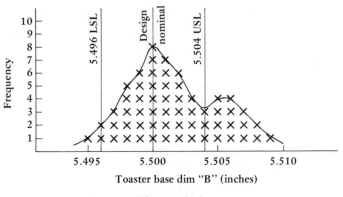

Figure 4–1

• The parts were made on two presses

• One press had a worn die

The die was replaced and process samples were randomly collected over the next operating shift. The parts were again measured and the results plotted as illustrated in Figure 4–2. The resulting graph showed parts that conformed to the specification and formed a nicely shaped bell curve.

The "normal" distribution shows that the unnatural factors (the worn die) have been removed and both presses are producing products "to spec."

Let's turn our attention to the topic of scientific discipline and discuss its importance and simplicity in process analysis and control.

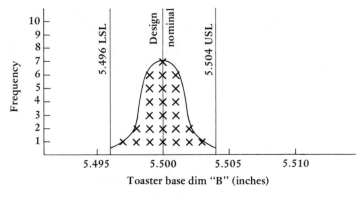

Figure 4–2

Scientific Discipline

Scientific discipline is nothing to be scared of. It simply takes the worry out of analyzing a problem by providing a simple and systematic way of looking at it. Remember always to follow the K.I.S.S. principle. Use of this simple discipline cannot be emphasized enough. You must avoid using the "shotgun" approach and resist trying to fit a solution to a problem. The scientific approach stops you from going about problem solving in the "Ready–Fire–Aim" mode.

The following four steps provide you with a simple basis for analyzing any process. They can be found in any elementary text that tells how to perform a scientific experiment. To do so, or to analyze a process, you simply:

1. Develop a hypothesis
2. Perform an experiment
3. Analyze the results
4. Draw appropriate conclusions

By following these four steps in the logical sequence, you can successfully solve problems and prevent their recurrence. Let's look at each step a bit more in depth to help you understand how simple and nonthreatening the process is.

To develop a hypothesis, you use brainstorming to yield a number of judgmental ideas about what you think the problem may be. These ideas are used to help you formulate a plan before you take action. This prevents you from "blowing off some toes before the gun clears the holster." In this stage, you must consider what you are going to measure and how it will be recorded. Complete definition of your plan and thorough understanding of environmental conditions is essential before taking any action.

Once the plan is well defined and understood you can safely begin the experimentation phase. Here it is most important to record all possible information associated with the problem— dates, time, lot number, operator(s), and material, to name a few. Since you don't yet know which ones are critical, you must be thorough and accurate. Be sure to record information concurrently so it can be "tied together" to construct a clear picture of what's happening. Waiting until later to correlate information will be too late. There is always something missing or you just won't get around it.

Data analysis is not always straightforward. Therefore, systematic analysis is critical if you are to obtain the most from your information. This is the critical point at which you must "let the data talk to you." Don't try to fit a preconceived resolution to a problem if the data says otherwise. Don't jump to conclusions. Take time to be certain you have done it right the first time. Repeat the experiment if necessary. One aid in listening effectively to your process is to ask "why" five times. Avoid asking "who." That will always cause conflict, which in turn may cause you to lose sight of your goal and waste valuable teamwork.

Having successfully completed the first three steps, you may now draw appropriate conclusions that are based on experimental information and not on speculation or hearsay. Comparison to the hypothesis will help you determine if your "judgment" call was correct or not. Whether or not you were correct, you will have arrived at a set of conclusions that can be used to take action to correct a situation and prevent its recurrence.

Let's look at an example as applied to a nonmanufacturing process. The incoming material screening or verification process must be directly linked to the process used to screen and select suppliers. Why? Because the validity of incoming material is directly associated with the ability of a supplier to produce a product or service which meets your specifications and expectations. This in turn is critical to the longevity and health of your business. The ultimate success of both customer and supplier is totally dependent on the supplier/customer relationship. Think about it!

If you don't follow a simple rigorous scientific logic when analyzing the capability of your business processes or those of your suppliers, you will be relying on blind luck. You don't want to run your business or your process that way, do you?

Specifications vs. Process Capability

Now it's time to examine and clarify the most often misunderstood and misinterpreted pair of terms: specifications and process capability

The objectives of this section are:

- To clarify the two terms
- To distinguish differences between the two
- To illustrate the relationship between them

Definitions

First, a *specification* is defined by Webster as:

A statement of particulars,
as of dimensions,
materials, etc.

Recall our definition of *process capability* in the previous section:

The natural or normal behavior of a process after the unnatural or abnormal disturbances affecting the process have been eliminated.

Examination of the definitions quickly shows that the two are distinctly different. However, the relationship between them is most important. Why? Because if a process isn't capable of producing products or services that meet the specification set by the customer, then we have a problem. Got the idea? Let's develop a hypothetical case to help you understand the differences and the relationship.

We will first create a hypothetical manufacturing process example and then examine an actual nonmanufacturing example.

Manufacturing Example

You own a small manufacturing business which supplies specialty fasteners to local auto parts houses and custom upholstery shops. One of your processes manufactures snaps for convertible tops and custom boat covers which have been a hot item this year. However, you have been receiving complaints from your prime customer that the snaps are either not remaining snapped or they are difficult to open.

When you review the situation with your manufacturing supervisor and machine operator you find they are able to produce the chart shown in Figure 4–3 for the male portion of the snap.

By plotting the outside diameters, recorded from the manufactured parts—in this case the critical mating surface—you were able to calculate the *control limits* and illustrate them as shown. When the part drawing was examined, the *design specification* for the critical diameter was found to be .501 ± .002. Plotting the spec's on the same chart as the control limits made it clear that the two did not agree. Furthermore, it was obvious why

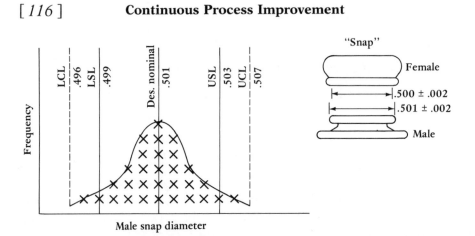

Male snap diameter

Figure 4–3

some snaps were not remaining snapped while others were difficult to open—that is, the diameter was in some cases too large and in others, too small.

Examination of the forming process led your operator to the following conclusions:

1. The recent set of dies received from ACME Tool and Die were not to your specification.
2. Some of your existing dies were found worn and producing parts larger than the spec called for.

Procurement Process Example

This example takes a second look at the case study in Chapter 1, where the procurement process required all material requests (MRs) to be coordinated and "approved" before they were released to the buyer or purchasing agent for processing. There was the perception that it always took too long to get anything through the procurement cycle.

The procurement process team decided to investigate the situation with the goal of alleviating the perception. The first thing they did was to gather and plot data showing how long it took to process an MR. Since they were not sure what they were looking for and they wanted to learn as much from process information as possible to avoid jumping to conclusions, they also plotted high dollar value vs. low dollar value, simple design vs. complex design, and overhead vs. directly applied costs. Data plotted in Figures 4–4(a) and 4–4(b) illustrates a ten-day median cycle time

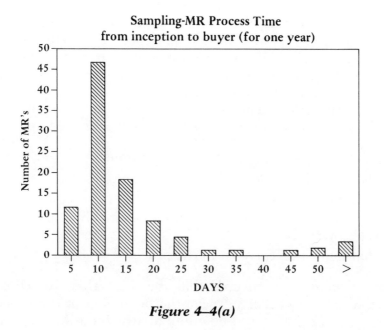

Figure 4–4(a)

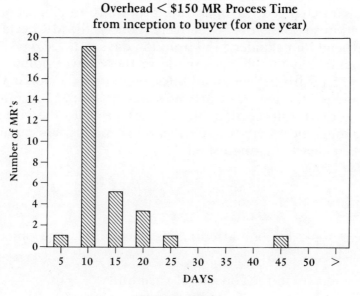

Figure 4–4(b)

for all MRs as well as those with a dollar value less than $150.

Even though there was no "design spec" for cycle time, the perception that it "took too long" was enough to proceed. Furthermore, the team decided that whatever the current cycle time came out to be, it had to be improved.

The team developed a process flow diagram for the procurement cycle. In their examination of the process they looked for:

- What took the longest time too accomplish?
- What added the least value?
- What was unnecessary?
- What could be eliminated without negatively impacting the cycle time?
- What happened early on in the process?

They ultimately discovered that the thing that was causing the greatest delay occurred near the beginning of the process, added no value, and could be eliminated without hurting cycle time. That one thing was a "preapproval" required by the finance department. With their PFD in hand, supported with hard data, the team marched off to see the finance manager. They were able to convince the finance manager that it would benefit everyone, including his staff, if the preapproval step were eliminated.

The team changed the operating procedure to eliminate that step, and in so doing, they effectively reduced the MR cycle time for overhead items under $150 from ten days to three days. They later found that the changes made to these lower dollar value MRs had a positive effect on all MRs, no matter the dollar value.

In this case, there were clearly no specs. Customer expectations were the driving force that brought attention to the situation. But the differences between specifications and process capability have been clearly distinguished.

Variability

The next topic for our attention is variability. The objectives are clearly:

- To understand the concept of variability
- To explore factors that contribute to variability

Definition

Webster defines *variable* as:

Tending to change; not constant; capable of being varied.

Variability is not something arcane or complex. Very simply, if something is variable, it is subject to change. When looking at a process, you will find variation that is inherent to the process and variation associated with the environment surrounding the process. It is important to distinguish between the two because you can usually do something about the former type while the latter is sometimes difficult to change or control. For example, it is relatively easy to control the speed at which some product or service is performed or delivered. However, it may be a more challenging task to maintain constant temperature and relative humidity surrounding a process. You might think that the thermostat on the wall was put there to control the heating and air conditioning output temperature. You will never convince me that that is true!

Factors Contributing to Variability

As you might imagine, a multitude of factors can affect a process and contribute to its variability. Consider the temperature change from season to season in a machine shop without air conditioning and the effect it could have on part dimensions. Or what about the environmental impact of moving a distribution warehouse and personnel from Baton Rouge, Louisiana to Hartford, Connecticut. Basically, all contributing factors can be grouped into five simple categories. Remember the 5Ms from Chapter 3? Figure 4–5 is a reminder of how all the pieces fit together.

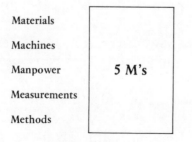

Figure 4–5

Now that you have made the link between the 5Ms and variability, the only thing left to do is link the 5Ms to the root cause. By performing that step we will have made a direct connect between variability and root cause. Furthermore, we have a way of categorically analyzing the various elements. Pretty neat trick, don't you think?

EXERCISE

As a team, take a few moments and brainstorm how each of the 5Ms can affect your process. Discuss and record your findings. Remember to follow the ground rules.

Variability and Control

This section is designed to put the concept of variability into action by associating it with process control. The objectives are:

- To help you understand what can and should be controlled
- To develop an understanding of natural and unnatural variation and show you how to recognize the difference

Definitions

The following six working definitions are included as a basis for discussion of this topic.

Natural variation: The pattern produced by plotting a random set of data collected from a process affected by no abnormal disturbances.

Unnatural variation: The pattern that results from plotting data produced by a process that is affected by abnormal disturbances.

Control: Exercise power over; restrain; govern; dominate; regulate; verify by comparison. This can be a customer or user constraint.

Statistics: The science of collecting and interpreting numerical data.

Common cause: Random, natural causes associated with a process that require no corrective or preventive action.

Special cause: Nonrandom causes associated with a process or process environment that require corrective and/or preventive action.

Variation, Feedback, and Control

The two types of variation associated with a process have been defined here as *natural* and *unnatural*. Understanding the difference between the two will help you understand how to interpret the performance of a process. Data collection and interpretation and feedback mechanisms are used to monitor critical characteristics within a process to help you identify the changes caused by unnatural disturbances. Recognizing and interpreting changes through the use of control charts, which operate on the fundamental principles of statistics and natural variation, enable you to recognize when unnatural variation is present so that the source (root cause) can be identified and eliminated before a problem occurs.

From a broad business perspective, process interaction and feedback mechanisms are essential if customers are to be satisfied and a business is to remain healthy and profitable. To illustrate this point, let's examine a few hypothetical situations which may cause some of you to flinch when you read them. They are perhaps too close to reality.

Suppose an engineering design was completed without input to or feedback from manufacturing, materials, or shop operations. Chances are the design would not be manufactured on time, or to design spec, and possibly it wouldn't be completed at all. Therefore, it is vital that timely and meaningful dialogue occurs between the design function, the manufacturing organization, and other support functions to ensure the product can be made with existing processes or with a process designed specifically for that purpose.

If a procurement operation is not given copies of design specs and manufacturing schedules as part of their procurement instructions, they will not be able to order material to be delivered at required intervals nor will they be able to negotiate prices at competitive levels. Therefore, the procurement operation *must* be integrated into the design and manufacturing information channels at an early and appropriate time.

If the price quoted to a potential customer has not taken the engineering organization or the manufacturing schedules into account, it might well be too low to cover the customer's functional requirements, or there could be no room in the manufacturing schedule.

If any of these situations rings a bell, it's probable that your business processes have not been properly integrated or are ill equipped with proper feedback mechanisms to help preclude such occurrences. What all of these examples have in common is that no one took time to *listen* to what processes had to tell them.

Characteristics of Natural Variation

Identical twins are not identical. Two cars with identical specifications are not identical. Two parallel processes are not identical, nor will they produce identical products. Why? Because there is variation in everything we make or do. Even things that appear to be identical have minute but significant differences that could eventually have an adverse affect on a business process.

If the variation in your process occurs more or less by chance, in a random fashion, and is an inherent part of the process, then it is considered to be *natural.* If you were to select a particular process indicator, record it over a period of time, and then chart the measurements, you would find that the measurements varied about a middle value and were evenly distributed. You would notice also that the data formed a bell-shaped curve commonly referred to as a "normal" distribution curve.

A normal distribution curve has three distinct characteristics that make it a valuable tool in understanding and controlling processes. They are:

- Consistent shape
  - Usually bell-shaped
  - Not bimodal or skewed (but symmetrical)
  - Predictable (doesn't change with time)

- Consistent center
  - Stable
  - Does not fluctuate
  - Predictable

- Consistent spread
  - Stable
  - Does not fluctuate
  - Predictable

Take a look at the graphical representation in Figure 4–6 to ensure you have a clear picture of a normal distribution curve.

As you will see later in this chapter, the normal distribution curve provides the basis for construction and interpretation of control charts.

The Relationship Between Control and Capability

In order fully to understand and interpret process activity, you must have a firm grasp of the differences between process capability and process control. Why? Because:

- A process can be out of control but still be capable of meeting customer specifications.
- A process can also be in control and not be able to meet customer specs.
- A process can be in control and meet specs (this of course is the preferred condition).

This topic has always presented a challenge to anyone who tried to explain it clearly. Robert Piselli, whose expertise in statistical process control is matched by his extraordinary graphic ability to make complex phenomena simple, developed the matrix shown in Figure 4–7. You will find this matrix a very handy reference tool as you become more of a statistical thinker.

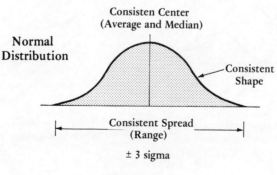

Figure 4–6

Roll-the-Dice Exercise

This exercise will give you an idea of the "odds" you are up against in a Las Vegas or Atlantic City casino when you play any game using dice. If you had never examined a pair of dice, you probably wouldn't know what to expect. Well, if you were to roll a pair of dice, the most probable combination to appear would add up to seven. What do you think the probability would be for you to roll "box cars" or "snake eyes"? Try rolling the dice 50 times, record the results on a chart, and see what happens.

If you would like to add some fun and diversion to the exercise, consider using a pair of loaded dice. By introducing one set of loaded dice into a group where five teams are rolling dice and recording results, you will get at least one set of unexpected results. This gives you the opportunity to stress the value of using

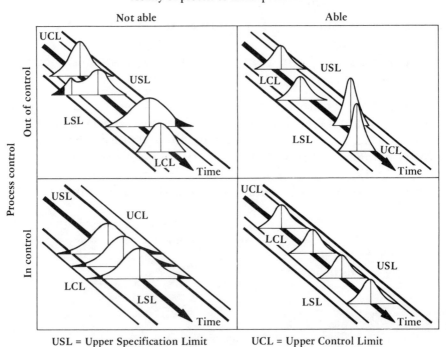

Ability of process to meet specification limits

USL = Upper Specification Limit   UCL = Upper Control Limit
LSL = Lower Specification Limit   LCL = Lower Control Limit

Figure 4–7(a)

REPRINTED BY PERMISSION OF GENERAL ELECTRIC.

Ability of process to meet specification limits

	Not able	Able
Out of control	• Inconsistent shape of distribution • Inconsistent process center • Inconsistent process spread • Exceeds specification limits • Not predictable	• Inconsistent shape of distribution • Inconsistent process center • Inconsistent process spread • Consistently within the specification limits • Not predictable
In control	• Consistent shape of distribution • Consistent process center • Consistent process spread • Exceeds specification limits • Predictable	• Consistent shape of distribution • Consistent process center • Consistent process spread • Consistently within the specification limits • Predictable

(Process control)

Figure 4–7(b)

REPRINTED BY PERMISSION OF GENERAL ELECTRIC.

the 5Ms to analyze what might be wrong. Let's see how it actually worked with a group of managers in Canada.

Five team members were asked to perform the experiment. Four sets of results were quite similar and looked much like the bell curve they had just discussed. However, one member's results caused the central part of the curve to skew nearer to 12 than 7. When asked "What do you suppose happened to affect your results?" no one was able to produce an explanation. However, when they used the 5Ms in the following manner, they were able to arrive at the correct conclusion.

- *Machines:* The first M was ruled out of the process because they had not used any mechanical device to roll the dice.
- *Methods:* The effect of the second M was discounted because the same method was used to roll the dice each time, i.e. they were rolled on a flat table without impacting any vertical surface.

- *Manpower:* The third M was negated because there was no change in manpower, i.e. the same person rolled the dice each time.
- *Measurement:* Impact of the fourth M was ruled out because they figured that all addition had been done correctly.
- *Materials:* Examination of the last M led them to question whether or not there was something wrong with the dice.

As you can see, analysis using the 5Ms gave the management team a systematic means of looking for the root cause of the problem.

Control Charts

Most people approach control charts with little knowledge of the subject and much trepidation. The objective of this section is to familiarize you with the basic types of control charts and their simple application. To accomplish this we will address three topics:

- What is a control chart?
- Constructing a control chart
- Basic types of control charts

A discussion about what control charts are will help remove the mystique.

What Is a Control Chart?

Control charts are a link between you and your process that allows you to "keep your finger on the pulse" and "dialogue" with your process. Since dialoguing is such an important part of problem solving, understanding and knowing how to use control charts to your advantage is vital.

If you locate the measurement points on your PFD, you will have identified the "pulse" locations of your process. Since you can dialogue with your process at these critical locations, through "listening" and analysis you can:

- Recognize changes to a process
- Identify changes within a process

- Monitor and evaluate improvement actions
- See trends to help keep your process in control
- Prevent your process from making bad products or supplying bad services

Since control charts are based on the statistical principle of normal distribution, you must understand how they are constructed so they can be analyzed and interpreted to your advantage.

Constructing a Control Chart

Repeat the dice rolling exercise and collect and plot your data in the following manner:

1. Use the chart pictured in Figure 4–8 to plot the dice totals for each of the 50 throws.

   Think of the horizontal lines as strings and the data you collect as beads. Now, as you roll the dice and add up the total, place a bead on the appropriate string indicating the dice total and slide it to the left until you reach the time location at which you made the measurement. Suppose you first rolled a total of 4. A bead would be placed on the fourth string and slid to the left to the appropriate time position. The second total rolled happened to be 7. The same procedure would be followed to locate the second bead on the seventh string and just to the right of the first bead.

2. Using the same procedure, record 100 dice rolls on the chart. If you actually did this, you would end up with a chart

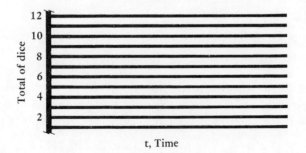

Figure 4–8

with 100 beads located at 100 consecutive points along the horizontal axis. The question now is how does this relate to a control chart or a normal distribution curve?

3. To make the connection with a normal distribution curve, rotate the chart so the "strings" are oriented vertically on the page. This will allow the beads to fall toward the bottom of the page creating a "bell" shaped curve.

If you think of data collection and display in this manner, you will always be able to visualize the continuous building of a normal distribution curve. Later as you learn about control limits and other control chart characteristics, this will provide a reference for you to build and visualize new information.

Basic Types of Control Charts

There are only two basic types of control charts, *attribute* charts and variable charts. Attribute charts are used to display and analyze data characterized as:

- Good or bad
- Yes or no
- Pass or fail
- Go or no-go

Attribute data is the type of information you would expect to gather from inspection sheets. It is usually data found in files, though sometimes it is never recorded but characterized by bins full of scrap or parts that "don't meet spec." Some examples of attribute data are:

- Shipment was on time or late
- Surface had bubbles
- Routing form was complete or incomplete
- Customer was satisfied or dissatisfied.

Variable data, on the other hand, gives an indication of how much or to what extent something is happening. A few examples of variable information might be:

- Number of shipments leaving the warehouse per hour
- pH of a chemical mixture

- Turn time
- Physical dimensions
- Environmental conditions

If this is not totally clear at this point, be patient with yourself. The examples and explanations that follow will help clarify your questions. Should you wish to go into more depth on the subject, it is suggested that you refer to a text on statistical process control.

Although there are only two basic types of control charts, these two categories can be further expanded into the chart variations presented below:

Attribute Charts
np
p
c
u

Variable Charts
x, R
$\bar{x}$, R
$\tilde{x}$, R

Although there are seven different charts to choose from, we will focus on only one attribute chart (c chart) and one variable chart (x and R chart). These two will help you understand how to construct an actual control chart. Selection of a chart for a specific application is a bit more complex. Therefore, that discussion will be deferred until later in this chapter.

Before getting into the detail of chart construction, we need to address one more chart characteristic: i.e. control limits.

Control Limits

The objectives of this topic are:

- To introduce you to the concept of control limits
- To help you understand what control limits are and what they are not.

- To show you how to calculate and locate control limits on a control chart

Let's start with a brief discussion of what they are.

What Are Control Limits?

Think of your PFD as a road map and picture yourself in a car. As you drive from operation to operation you need to be sure you stay on the road and don't get surprised by a detour or other obstacle. Control limits are visual aids to help you read your map so you:

- Know where you have been
- Know where you are
- Know where you are going
- Stay on the road
- Avoid detours
- Avoid accidents

Moving away from the metaphor and into the language of your process, control limits let you know where your process was, is, and is going.

They also assist you in determining if, and how much, your process is varying.

What They Are Not

Control limits are *not* specification limits. Control limits are a function of the process and specification limits are created by customer needs and expectations. In other words, process control limits are *not* dependent on the specification limits set by a product or process design. Control limits let your process talk to you to tell you whether or not it can meet certain specifications. You learned earlier the distinction between specifications and the capability of a process. By putting these concepts together and understanding the differences and the connections you can use control charts to help ensure your processes remain in control and are capable of fulfilling customer expectations. Figure 4–9 should help clarify and enhance this discussion.

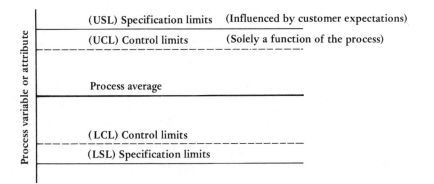

Figure 4–9

How Do You Calculate Control Limits?

Calculation of control limits is simple and straightforward. All you need is some basic information available from your process and a few constants available from any statistical process control reference text. In this case you will be given the basic equations for calculation of upper control limits (UCL) as well as lower control limits (LCL). All constants required are also provided in tabular form so that there will be no need for you to go searching for a reference.

The equations for calculating UCLs and LCLs are presented in Figures 4–10 and 4–11, which were adapted to this text from course material developed by GE. The tabular form provides you with all equations and constants to calculate control limits for all seven types of charts listed earlier.

Simple substitution of appropriate constants, based on process information, enable the simple calculations to be completed and the results to be plotted on the control chart. The examples and exercises included in the next section will give you an opportunity to perform these calculations and plot the resultant control limits.

Practical Use of Control Charts

The information and exercises in this section will:

- Familiarize you with the basic types of control charts
- Provide you with a basic understanding of when, where, and how to use these charts

ATTRIBUTE CONTROL LIMITS

CHART	DESCRIPTION	SAMPLE SIZE (N)	CONTROL LIMITS	
			SIMPLIFIED	COMPLETE
NP	NUMBER OF DEFECTIVE UNITS	CONSISTENT/EQUAL	$\pm 3\sqrt{N\overline{P}}$	$\pm 3\sqrt{N\overline{P}(1-N\overline{P}/N)}$
P	PERCENT DEFECTIVE $P = \dfrac{\text{TOTAL DEFECTIVE}}{\text{SAMPLE SIZE}}$	VARIES	$\pm 3\sqrt{\overline{P}/N}$	$\pm 3\sqrt{[\overline{P}(1-\overline{P})]/N}$
U	DEFECTS PER UNIT $u = \dfrac{\text{TOTAL DEFECTIVE}}{\text{SAMPLE SIZE}}$	VARIES	$\pm 3\sqrt{\overline{u}/N}$	$\pm 3\sqrt{\overline{u}/N}$
C	DEFECTS PER UNIT $c = \dfrac{\text{TOTAL DEFECTIVE}}{\text{SAMPLE SIZE}}$	CONSISTENT/EQUAL	$\pm 3\sqrt{\overline{C}}$	$\pm 3\sqrt{\overline{C}}$

Figure 4–10

VARIABLE CONTROL CHART LIMITS

CHART	DESCRIPTION	CENTER LINE	CONTROL LIMITS	STANDARD FACTORS			
X, R	INDIVIDUALS	$\overline{X} = \Sigma X/N$ $\overline{R} = \Sigma R/N$	UCL, LCL $= \overline{X} \pm E_2\overline{R}$ UCL $= \overline{R}\,D_4$ LCL $= \overline{R}\,D_3$	n	E_2	D_4	D_3
				2	2.66	3.27	0
				3	1.77	2.57	0
				4	1.46	2.28	0
				5	1.29	2.11	0
$\overline{X}$, R	AVERAGES	$\overline{\overline{X}} = \Sigma X/N$ $\overline{R} = \Sigma R/N$	UCL, LCL $= \overline{\overline{X}} \pm A_2\overline{R}$ UCL $= \overline{R}\,D_4$ LCL $= \overline{R}\,D_3$	n	A_2	D_4	D_3
				2	1.88	3.27	0
				3	1.02	2.57	0
				4	0.73	2.28	0
				5	0.58	2.11	0
$\widetilde{X}$, R	MEDIANS	$\widetilde{\overline{\overline{X}}} = $ MIDDLE $\widetilde{X}$ $\overline{R} = \Sigma R/N$	UCL, LCL $= \widetilde{\overline{\overline{X}}} \pm \widetilde{A}_2\overline{R}$ UCL $= \overline{R}\,D_4$ LCL $= \overline{R}\,D_3$	n	$\widetilde{A}_2$	D_4	D_3
				2	1.88	3.27	0
				3	1.19	2.57	0
				4	0.80	2.28	0
				5	0.69	2.11	0

n = # of Samples Within a Subgroup
N = # of Subgroups

Figure 4–11

- Eliminate the mystery and trepidation associated with the use and selection of control charts

These objectives will be accomplished by discussing the following topics:

- Construction and use of the c chart
- Construction and use of the x, R chart
- Selecting the right chart
- Interpretation
- Out-of-control conditions
- The flip of a coin
- Processes out of control
- Assignable cause
- Calculating new control limits

Construction and Use of the c Chart

The c chart is an attribute chart used to monitor nonconformities in a process sample. It enables you to classify physical characteristics as either good or bad. In this case, you are looking for things that are bad, because a nonconformity is simply something that does not meet customer expectations or the specifications for the process in question. Like all control charts, the c chart is used in special circumstances. The one and only environmental and process characteristic that must be present to use the c chart is that *the sample size must remain constant*—it cannot change at any time in the monitoring process. The c chart can be used in either high- or low-volume processes. The control limits are easily calculated.

Let's see how it works by actually constructing a chart. The following steps can be used any time you wish to construct a c chart and calculate control limits.

1. Begin by ensuring the sample size is constant.
2. Next, count and record the number of nonconformities in each sample.
3. Plot the recorded data on a chart prepared for attribute data. Plot it in time order so you can relate the occurrences to historical events.

4. Connect the points with a solid continuous line.
5. After you have plotted at least 10, and preferably 25 points, calculate the average (this is called $\bar{c}$) using the equation:

$$\bar{c} = (c_1 + c_2 + c_3 + \ldots + c_N)/N$$

6. Draw a horizontal solid line on the chart and mark it as $\bar{c}$.
7. Calculate the control limits using the following equations:

$$UCL = \bar{c} + 3 \sqrt{\bar{c}}$$

$$LCL = \bar{c} - 3 \sqrt{\bar{c}}$$

8. Construct the control limits using broken lines and mark them appropriately as UCL and LCL.

Suppose you and your team are part of a customer service organization that records and coordinates customer problems. You have a standard form on which service specialists record pertinent data to help identify the problems. There have been complaints from the engineering and manufacturing divisions that the forms have not been properly completed by your team. This has hindered problem resolution and is causing unnecessary delays in identifying and reporting corrective action to your customers.

To help correct the situation, you decided to monitor the complaint form by using a c chart to plot the number of incomplete items found on each form. Since you process approximately six customer complaints each day, recording the missing information for one week should give you a reasonable representation of what's happening.

The tabulation on page 135 represents the number of missing items on each form.

By transferring the tabulated data to a c chart, you can quickly see the magnitude of the situation. A simple calculation shows that on the average there are 3.1 items left incomplete when the form leaves customer service.

Two more calculations produce control limits which are easily plotted:

$$UCL = 8.38$$

$$LCL = -2.18$$

Form	#Missing Items	Form	#Missing Items
1	3	15	5
2	7	16	7
3	4	17	0
4	2	18	0
5	6	19	3
6	5	20	1
7	0	21	8
8	2	22	4
9	1	23	4
10	0	24	2
11	2	25	0
12	3	26	6
13	5	27	3
14	1		

In this case, the lower control limit is discarded because it is impossible to have a less than zero defect rate on an attribute chart.

This simple example shows how to construct a c chart. Contrary to popular belief, use of control charts is not limited to manufacturing processes. In this example, the message to the customer support organization is clear: completion of all forms makes everyone's job easier. Copy the blank c chart in Figure 4–12 and plot all the information ascribed to this customer support situation.

Remember that any nonconformity can be charted on a c chart if you can establish a standard sample size. The nonmanufacturing example illustrates just one possible use. A little imagination on your part can uncover additional applications such as:

- Number of times a drawing required a revision
- The number of discrepancies on a drawing
- The number of checks returned for missing signatures

Use of the c chart is straightforward and simple. Later in the chapter we will discuss how to interpret information plotted on the chart. The most important thing to recognize at this point is that all the data should fall within the control limits. If they don't, then you have an opportunity for process improvement.

Control Chart for Attribute Data

Part/Asm Name		Operation		Nonconforming Units	Nonconformities	Chart No.	
Part No.		Department		☐ np	☐ c	Average Sample Size	
Parameter		Specification		☐ p	☐ u	Frequency	

	Sample Size (n)																								
Discrep-tancies	Number (np, c)																								
	Proportion (p.u.)																								
	Date																								

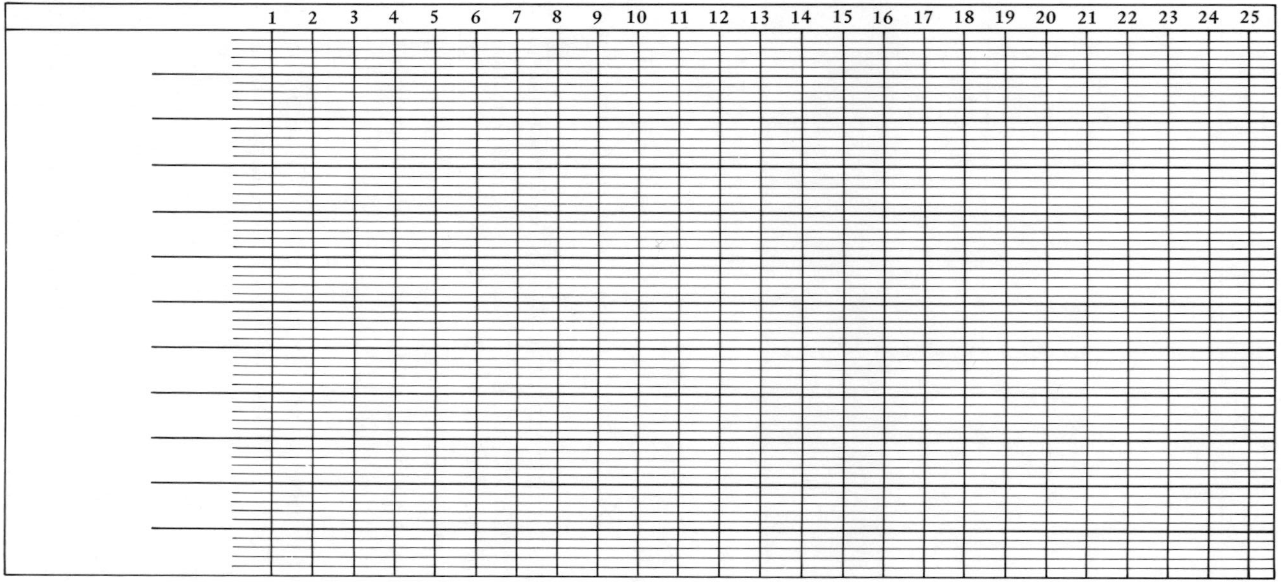

Figure 4–12. c Chart

[*136*]

Construction and Use of the x, R Chart

The (x, R) chart is used to plot and interpret data that help you understand and use the critical variables in your process. As I mentioned before, variable data tells you how much or to what extent the process is changing versus whether the outcome is good or bad. Use of this type of chart can help prevent making a bad product or providing an unsuitable service. This chart is particularly valuable when measurements are expensive, cause the product to be destroyed, or cause delays in the service rendered.

Let's see what it takes to construct and use an x, R chart.

1. Begin by establishing a start date and sequential time line for events to be recorded "as they occur" on the x-axis.
2. The vertical line on the chart is used to relate the time sequence of events to the items that vary and to calculate and plot the range (R) between consecutive data points. A good rule of thumb to apply here is to make the y-axis scale 1.5 times the range of data. This will help avoid replotting data because your scale was too small.
3. Plot the data points on the X chart in chronological sequence and connect the points with a series of straight solid lines.
4. Calculate the difference between successive data points and then plot them on the range chart. There will be one less point on the range chart than there is on the X chart because you are calculating the difference between successive data points. Complete the R chart by connecting the points with a series of straight lines. The example will help clarify this.
5. After you have plotted at least 25 points on the X chart, use the following formulas to calculate the average for both charts:

   $$\bar{X} = X \text{ avg} = (X1 + X2 + X3 + X4 + \ldots + XN)/N$$

   $$\bar{R} = R \text{ avg} = (R1 + R2 + R3 + R4 + \ldots + RN-1)/(N-1)$$

   Since R avg is based on the difference between successive values of X, the denominator reflects a value one less than the total number of data points, i.e., $X - 1$.

6. Now display the average values on the appropriate charts with a solid line on each.

7. Calculate the control limits for the X portion and the R portion using the formulas and constants from Figure 4–11.

Now that you have all the steps required to construct an x, R chart, let's look at an example from an actual process to see what a completed chart really looks like.

It is common practice for parts susceptible to surface corrosion or attack from environmental elements to be protected by a coating. A common means of applying such a coating is through anodizing. This process includes electrolytic deposition of a material on the surface to be protected. The thickness of the deposit is the critical parameter in this process and is the variable chosen for this example.

Ten data points were collected over a period of weeks and were plotted on the chart in Figure 4–13. The dates the data was collected are shown on the chart along with the calculated range values. The averages and control limits were calculated and plotted as shown. Note that on the range chart, LCL = 0 in all cases because the difference between successive points can never be less than zero.

As you will soon learn, this process depicted on the chart is in control. And as you can see from the position of the spec limits, the process is capable of producing products within specification.

No further interpretation of the data is discussed at this point because the sole purpose of the example is to illustrate the basic construction of the x, R chart.

These charts have application possibilities limited only by:

• The rules governing each chart
• Your imagination to apply them

The secret to using any control chart is selection of the critical characteristics that affect and control the output of the process. The place to look for them is your PFD. Some examples of critical parameters might be:

• Fluid viscosity
• Chemical pH
• Film thickness

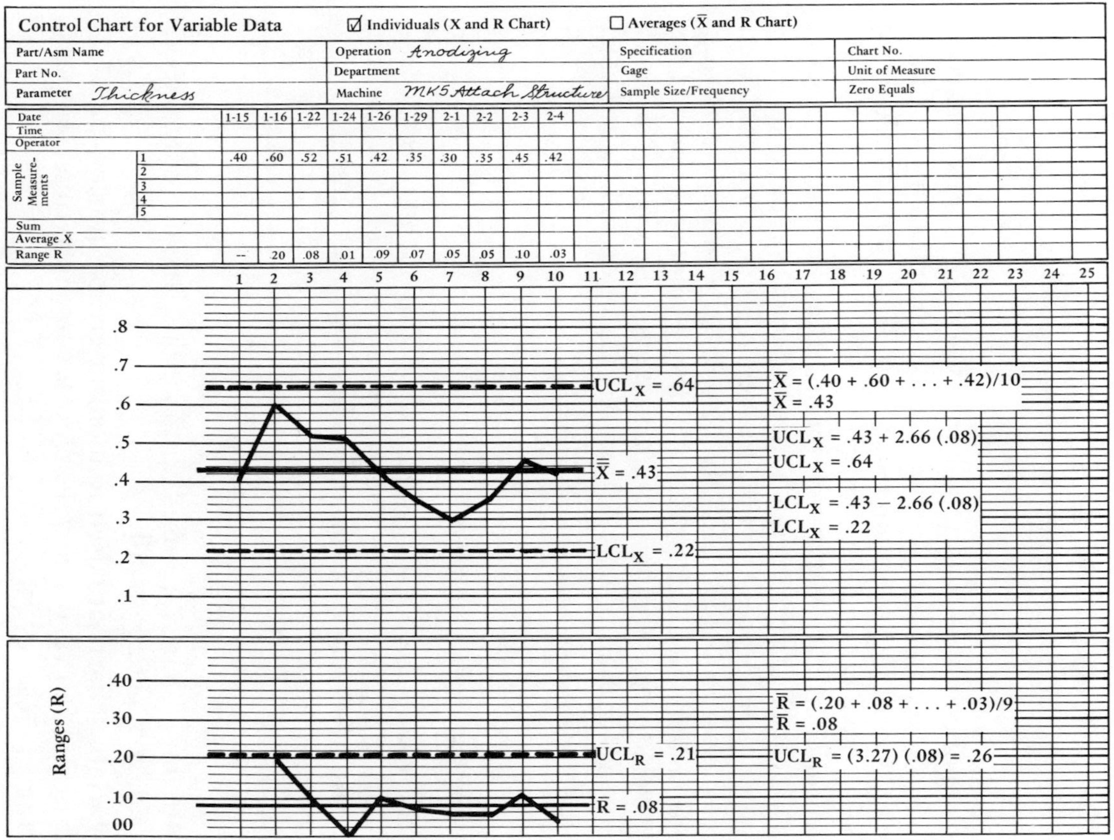

Control Chart for Variable Data

☑ Individuals (X and R Chart)　　☐ Averages (X̄ and R Chart)

Part/Asm Name		Operation	Anodizing		Specification		Chart No.
Part No.		Department			Gage		Unit of Measure
Parameter	Thickness	Machine	MK5 Attach Structure		Sample Size/Frequency		Zero Equals

Date	1-15	1-16	1-22	1-24	1-26	1-29	2-1	2-2	2-3	2-4
Time										
Operator										
Sample Measurements 1	.40	.60	.52	.51	.42	.35	.30	.35	.45	.42
2										
3										
4										
5										
Sum										
Average X̄										
Range R	--	.20	.08	.01	.09	.07	.05	.05	.10	.03

$$\bar{\bar{X}} = (.40 + .60 + \ldots + .42)/10$$
$$\bar{\bar{X}} = .43$$
$$UCL_X = .43 + 2.66\,(.08)$$
$$UCL_X = .64$$
$$LCL_X = .43 - 2.66\,(.08)$$
$$LCL_X = .22$$

$UCL_X = .64$

$\bar{\bar{X}} = .43$

$LCL_X = .22$

$$\bar{R} = (.20 + .08 + \ldots + .03)/9$$
$$\bar{R} = .08$$
$$UCL_R = (3.27)\,(.08) = .26$$

$UCL_R = .21$

$\bar{R} = .08$

Ranges (R)

Figure 4-13

- Number of incomplete repair procedures
- Number of late customer shipments
- Time to process a customer repair
- Time to process repair paperwork
- Time to submit a request for quotation

One final condition to remember in the use of control charts—K.I.S.S. Never make it difficult. If it's complex, try to find a simpler way of looking at the situation. If it's too complex, you probably have bitten off too much to chew.

Control charts are not an end point. They are simply a set of tools to be used at appropriate times and under proper conditions to enable your process to talk to you. It's up to you and your process team to listen carefully to what the process is saying. Careful listening will often reveal things you never expected.

We've listed seven different charts, each with a set of "proper" conditions for their use. Let's turn our attention to how to select the proper chart for a given occasion.

Selecting the Right Chart

Selection of the proper chart is not a difficult or complex process. By following some simple guidelines and through practice and application, selection of the right chart becomes second nature. Just remember to think logically and collect all the facts possible before choosing.

Recalling our earlier discussion:

- Attribute charts are used to monitor attribute data—good/bad, go/no-go, pass/fail.
- Variable charts are used to monitor critical process parameters that can vary—thickness, cycle time, turn time, temperature.

The following matrix was adapted from a GE reference text and is a handy tool to keep at your fingertips. It's recommended that you keep a copy with your PFD so the selection process can be done in concert with your process environment.

Attributes Chart	Description	Sample Size
np	Number of defective units in a sample	Equal/consistent
p	Percent defective in a sample	Varies
c	Number of defects in a sample	Equal/consistent
u	Number of defects per unit	Varies

Variables Chart	Description	General Use
x	Individuals	Low volume, destructive testing
$\bar{X}$	Averages	High volume, multiple measurements computer applications. High reliability indicator
$\tilde{X}$	Medians	Medium to high volume, quick and simple applications.

Interpretation

Now that you have experienced the process of selecting, constructing, and using two control charts, you have the basic knowledge to use both attribute and variable charts as the need arises. However, the charts are no good to you unless you can truly *listen* to what they are trying to tell you. Let's see what it takes to interpret control chart results and put them to use to your advantage.

The objectives of this subsection are:

- To show you how to interpret the results plotted on a control chart
- To help you understand how you can quickly recognize the need for corrective and preventive action
- To help you understand why certain conditions indicate a process is out of control.

Let's begin by examining some conditions that indicate a process is out of control.

OUT-OF-CONTROL CONDITIONS

Some simple rules will help you understand and recognize when your process is out of control or on its way. Besides following some basic statistical principles, they are pretty much common sense. Three general rules should be remembered. A process is considered to be out of control when:

1. A significant change is evident
2. The "process center" has shifted
3. Unnatural variation is apparent

The first two will probably be pretty evident to the casual untrained observer but the third requires a bit of statistical background.

The following table will help illustrate and simplify the statistical part of the process. You will notice the resemblance to a control chart with three zones superimposed for demonstration purposes. Referring to the table you will know that unnatural variation is present when:

- Any point occurs outside of the control limits
- There are two out of three successive points in Zone A or beyond.
- Four out of five consecutive points fall in Zone B or beyond.
- Eight consecutive points occur on one side of the centerline.

The following figures are reprinted with permission from GE to illustrate some commonly encountered control chart patterns.

Upper Control Limit	
Zone A	+3 sigma
Zone B	+2 sigma
Zone C	+1 sigma
————Center Line————	
Zone C	−1 sigma
Zone B	−2 sigma
Zone A	−3 sigma
Lower Control Limit	

Pattern   Interpretation

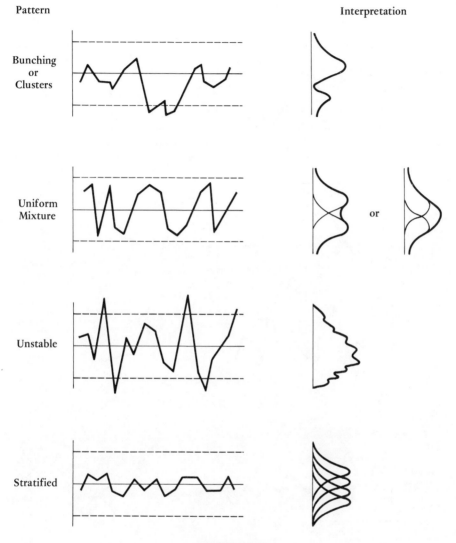

Figure 4–14
REPRINTED BY PERMISSION OF GENERAL ELECTRIC.

Each pattern is accompanied by a distribution curve to illustrate the variation from a bell curve.

The Flip of a Coin

No, this is not a management decision-making exercise, but you probably never expected to turn such a simple activity into a technique to help interpret control chart activity.

Pattern   Interpretation

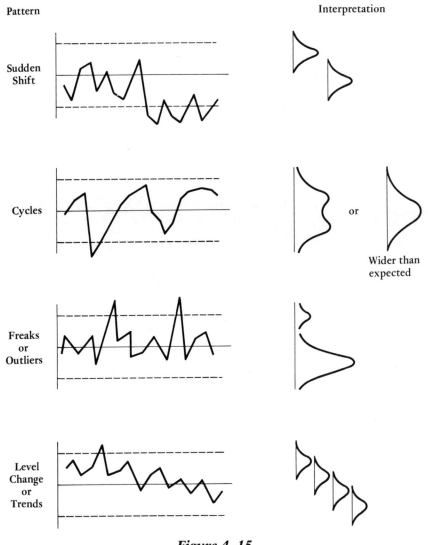

Figure 4–15
REPRINTED BY PERMISSION OF GENERAL ELECTRIC.

If you refer back to the conditions for unnatural variation, you may ask why the four conditions described there are valid indicators for out-of-control conditions. Looking at the condition described as "eight consecutive points on one side of the center-line," you can find validation based on statistical probability. This is where the flip of a coin can really tell you a lot.

Take out a coin and try this experiment.

Pattern   Interpretation

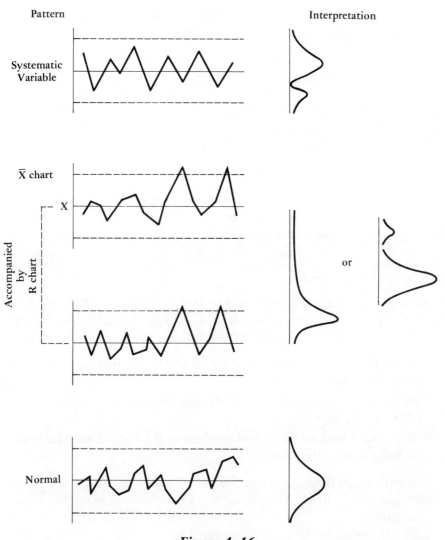

Figure 4–16
REPRINTED BY PERMISSION OF GENERAL ELECTRIC.

1. What is the probability of flipping the coin and having it come up "heads"? Answer: 50% or 0.50.
2. What is the probability of flipping the coin again and having it come up "heads" a second consecutive time? Answer: .50 × .50 = .25 or 25%.
3. What would be the probability of getting "heads" the third time? Answer: .50 × .50 × .50 = .125 or 12.5%. This means

you would have about 12 chances out of 100 of flipping "heads" three times in a row. Not very good odds.

Now that you have the idea, try getting eight consecutive points to appear on the same side of the centerline of a process without some unnatural variation "helping you." That's the same as trying to flip "heads" eight times in a row without trying to control or time the flipping sequence.

If you take the time to figure the probability you get:

$$.5 \times .5 \times .5 \times .5 \times .5 \times .5 \times .5 \times .5 = 0.004 \ (.4\%)$$

That's 4 chances in 1,000! So you can see why eight points in a row on one side of a process centerline is probably good cause to say your process is out of control.

Processes out of Control

Now that you have a comfortable feel for identifying whether or not a process is out of control, it's time to help you figure out what to do next. The objectives of this subsection are:

- To help you determine what to do after finding out that your process is out of control.
- To associate the concept of "assignable cause" with an out-of-control process.
- To explain how to calculate new control limits after eliminating the assignable cause(s).

We will begin by answering the question, "OK, now that we've identified a condition that appears to be out of control, what do we do?"

First, make sure that:

- Measurements are correct
- All measuring equipment is calibrated
- Data collection procedures were followed

Once that is done, you can begin to investigate the process for conditions that could cause it to be out of control. You might want to consider the following questions:

- What changed?
- Why did it change?

- Where did the change occur?
- What can be done to correct it?
- When?
- How do we prevent the condition from recurring?

Or in the case where a change resulted in a process improvement and you are not sure why, you will want to ask, "How do we make the change permanent?" In any event, *action* is required, but don't jump to conclusions. Remember to use discipline and logic when investigating the situation. It has paid off thus far. Don't stop now. You have all the tools you need to search for the assignable cause.

Assignable Causes

Don't panic. You will find out shortly that you have dealt with assignable causes already but they were called something different.

Begin by clearly marking the control chart where the out-of-control condition appears. This action instantly creates an historical record of when the situation occurred and where it happened. This is also an excellent point to begin your analysis because by looking at the data surrounding the out-of-control conditions, you might get some clues to help resolve your problem.

Now it's time to make use of the structure tree and to write a clear problem statement. Then apply the 5Ms to help identify the root cause of your problem. This disciplined activity will keep you focused on asking "Why?" and will avoid the killer "Who"?

Once you have identified the root cause, also known as the assignable cause, you can take appropriate steps to correct the condition and prevent recurrence.

Or, in the case of an improvement, you can:

- Upgrade the process by implementing the improvement.
- Change appropriate practices and procedures to institutionalize the change, i.e., make it permanent.

You shouldn't be the least bit surprised at the "continuous" application of tools such as the structure tree and the 5Ms. They are an integral part of the discipline and logic that make CPI a holistic business improvement system.

Calculating New Control Limits

When you have done something to change your process, you must determine what to do about the control limits. Why? Because any change in the process will most probably influence the control limits and thus must be accounted for so that future process control and analysis will be accurate and valid. When do you calculate the new limits?

In the last subsection you were instructed to mark the location of the out-of-control condition on the chart. This gives you a starting point to monitor the new process. However, you don't want to change or tamper with the control limits because you need to let the process stabilize before making any judgments. The same rule that applied to calculating the original control limits now applies to recalculation:

Recalculate new control limits only after at least 20 points, groups, or subgroups of data are available.

To assist in recalculation of control limits, some guidelines may be necessary. After an assignable cause has been removed and the process has been returned to operation, consider the following:

- Data points with assignable causes may be excluded from the control chart calculations. However, they represent historical information and must not be removed from the control chart.
- Recalculated process control limits must either be the same as the previous limits, or be narrower than the previous limits. Only under extraordinary circumstances would they increase.
- Consider a new process capability study if 20% or more points are being eliminated from the original process. Then consider calculating new control limits.
- After eliminating assignable causes and calculating new control limits, be very careful not to anticipate changes. Remember to allow the process to talk to you. Do not read in what is not there.

You now have all the tools and techniques that comprise CPI at your fingertips. You have seen them all in examples, in action on your own process, and have had the opportunity to use them all. The rest is all up to you! If you are an on-line contributing operator or the president or CEO of your company, you now have the tools to make this process work and become a living part of your business.

The tools are simple and the process is simple, but the implementation and change process requires a major commitment from the leaders of the business. By leaders, I don't necessarily mean the top-level managers who run the business. I really mean the people who are leaders. People like you who want to and can make a difference. You have the basic tools. The rest depends on you and your degree of *commitment*.

Real Time Application Assignment

You now have the opportunity to apply all you have learned and experienced. Use it to your advantage.

Using the data that you collected for your top problem in Chapter 3:

1. Select the type of chart that best fits your data
2. Plot the data on the selected chart
3. Calculate and plot control limits on your chart
4. Identify and illustrate spec limits associated with your process on the selected chart
5. Clearly identify the differences between *control limits* and *specification limits*

5

The Next Step

OK, where to now? The basic knowledge and fundamental use of the tools and techniques that make up CPI have been transferred to you and your team. You have had the opportunity to use each of them in classroom exercises and apply most of them to your natural work area. Your successes in improving your process were fun—even exhilarating—because you could fix or eliminate things that you and your team have long lived with, and you were able to accomplish this with the support of your management team. In the past this may have presented some difficulty because there was no direct association between what you were doing and the plans and goals of the business. However, using this methodology and open communication, you and your business management team have made it happen. Continuation of the dialogue is fundamental to taking the next step in the implementation and improvement process. The topics included in this chapter will prove invaluable in that effort. You will find some reminders related to information covered in earlier chapters as well as new topics to assist you in taking your next steps successfully.

The main topics to be addressed are:

- A few reminders
- Implementing corrective action
- Making a presentation
- Project requirements
- Team meetings
- The role of management
- Commitment

A Few Reminders

In keeping with the spirit of the previous chapters, take a few moments with your team to summarize what you have accomplished and learned since you began using CPI. Record key thoughts and comments and then spend some time discussing where you would be and what you might be doing had you not begun using the methodology.

Don't Jump to Conclusions

Recalling the basic principles of CPI from Chapter 1, problem prevention was second only to the methodology becoming a way of life. Systematic application of the tools and techniques you have acquired will help you avoid the tendency to jump to conclusions. The key steps involved in systematic problem resolution and prevention are included at this point to reemphasize their importance:

1. State the problem clearly
2. Test the statement for accuracy and clarity
3. Systematically search for root causes using the structure tree and the 5Ms
4. Establish and eliminate root cause
5. Implement corrective action to ensure recurrence is prevented
6. Install appropriate measurements to monitor preventive action
7. Change operating practices and measurements to ensure management systems support and institutionalize the "new" or "improved" process.

Continuous implementation of the CPI improvement system is a natural follow-through of the previous steps. As a matter of fact, they should form a continuum to move from the current process to the new or improved process. The CPI improvement wheel is shown once again (see Figure 5–1) as a reminder.

- Plan (study, analyze)
- Act (make it happen)
- Verify (test hypothesis)
- Institutionalize (change procedures, measurements, communicate)

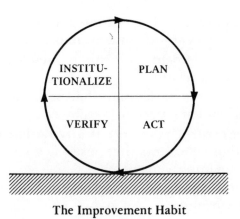

The Improvement Habit

Figure 5–1

REPRINTED BY PERMISSION OF GENERAL ELECTRIC.

Make Improvement a Continuous Process

The steps are simple to understand and follow. However, as you probably have already found out, it isn't easy to change from a reactive, bottom-line-focused operation to one committed to preventive, process-focused, bottom-line-aware, continuous improvement.

Continuous attention to the steps included in the implementation flow chart will help you make the change happen.

Implementing Corrective Action

Identifying corrective and preventive measures is a critical step in improving a process. However, without a well choreographed implementation plan, it is easy to get sidetracked and lose the short- and long-term benefits that can be realized from proper application. Therefore, we will spend some time addressing how to effectively implement and evaluate corrective action.

Develop an Effective Implementation Plan

I developed the following list over a two-year period while working with several businesses. Use the steps to develop an effective plan to implement and evaluate improvement actions.

1. Based on analysis and "environmental conditions," develop an effective, easy-to-implement plan.
2. Identify those elements of the plan intended to produce customer-oriented results.
3. Identify elements of the plan that pose the greatest risk to successful implementation.
4. Develop a control plan specifically designed to track and evaluate those elements that pose the greatest negative impact to your improvement plan.
5. Track and evaluate elements required to ensure superior process performance.
6. Analyze and evaluate current and past methods and systems affecting your process to understand:
   • What worked well
   • What didn't work well
   • Why the differences
   • How to benefit from both
7. Make your plan foolproof wherever and whenever possible.
8. Make your process people-independent; i.e., be able to answer "yes" to the question, "If the team members change, will the improved process remain improved and effective?"

Identify and Neutralize Resistance

Most people naturally resist change, no matter how beneficial it may be. Because there is bound to be resistance to your proposed changes, the following list is designed to help you identify and neutralize resistance. This should be used in conjunction with the forthcoming subsection, Potential Problem Prevention.

1. Brainstorm areas of the improvement plan that may encounter resistance.
2. Clearly identify where resistance may occur. Now is the time to ask *who* may cause the resistance.
3. Analyze why resistance might be encountered.
4. Formulate a plan to remove or neutralize the resistance so you can enter into a meaningful dialogue about the process.
5. Monitor your plan and its resisters for movement toward neutrality and buy-in.

Remember, when people can identify personal benefit from a change resistance is replaced with buy-in. Use this bit of knowledge to your advantage, along with the ownership test described in Chapter 1.

As exemplified through use of the ownership test, buy-in can be enhanced by:

- Participation
- Open communication
- Inviting people to become part of the solution (thus automatically ceasing to be part of the problem)

Measurements

We have already discussed the importance of measurements, possibly to the point of exhaustion. However, it is worth revisiting the subject in this context. Using the proper measurement at the proper time can mean the difference between successful implementation and rejection. Consider the following suggestions to use measurements to your advantage. Once you have determined what's critical to your process or improvement plan and have established specific goals:

1. Identify key characteristics to be measured
2. Establish appropriate units of measure
3. Develop a plan to collect measurements
4. Collect measurement data
5. Analyze and compare results to goals
6. Take appropriate action indicated

The importance of maintaining focus on team goals cannot be stressed enough. As one team member put it, "This allows us to maintain a link with our business's constancy of purpose statement."

Evaluate Impact

Early on in Chapter 3 you learned that the Pareto technique could help prioritize what to do first. You also learned that a Pareto evaluation must be performed after implementing corrective action because any change applied to one part of the process would have an effect on other parts of the process. There are special techniques, such as Taguchi, that can be used to evaluate several environmental variables at one time. We will briefly touch upon them at the end of this section. However, such activity is beyond the scope and simplicity of CPI and is left to the experts involved with selecting and implementing those practices and techniques.

A "world-class best practice" known as quality function deployment (QFD) utilizes a systematic rigor to evaluate the impact of a change on other parts of the process. A portion of that process was simplified and adapted for use as follows.

After using the abbreviated technique described here you may find the need for a more rigorous approach. In such a case, you are urged to seek assistance from an expert in whatever technique you choose.

1. Identify and record the critical process parameters in the space provided.
2. Using the judgment of your team, brainstorm the possible interacting effects of the parameters.
3. If you feel there will be a positive effect on parameter 1 by making a particular change to parameter 3, find the "diamond" created by the two intersecting diagonals (see Figure 5–2) and mark the space with a plus sign.
4. Similarly, mark a negative effect with a minus sign.

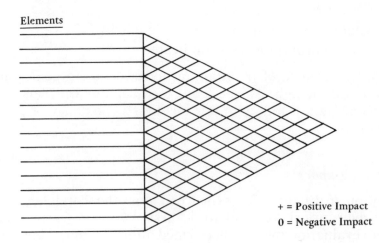

Elements

+ = Positive Impact
0 = Negative Impact

Figure 5–2

5. Use your judgments as part of the improvement implementation process to evaluate changes and their effects on other process parameters.

You are urged to create a form similar to that in Figure 5–2 to use in your analysis. Then consider linking it with the Nine Block to help you focus on what to do next with a bit less judgment and more analytical thinking.

Potential Problem Prevention

Potential problem prevention is a way of looking at root cause analysis in reverse. By foreseeing a problem that might occur and damage the improvement plan, you can move toward the root cause of the problem. Then by removing or neutralizing the root cause, the potential problem can be prevented or its effects neutralized. Let's see how it works.

1. Analyze each step in your implementation plan to determine whether there is a chance a problem could occur that could prevent your plan from succeeding or could negatively impact the results. Use Worksheet A (Figure 5–3) to record each potential problem. Rate the probability of occurrence and the seriousness of the problem as H, M, or L (high, medium, or low).
2. Use the Nine Block on Worksheet B (Figure 5–4) to identify the problems with the highest probability of occurrence and the highest potential to do the most damage to your plan.
3. Transfer the potential problems that fall in the H-H category to Worksheet C (Figure 5–5), the prevention structure tree.
4. Perform a potential problem analysis using the prevention structure tree and the 5Ms to identify the most probable root cause of the potential problem that could cause the most damage to your implementation plan.
5. Use Worksheet D (Figure 5–6) to record actions you need to take to prevent the potential problems from occurring or to neutralize the effects should they occur.

Implementation

Well, it's finally time to "press the start button." By now you should feel comfortable that most of the bases have been covered

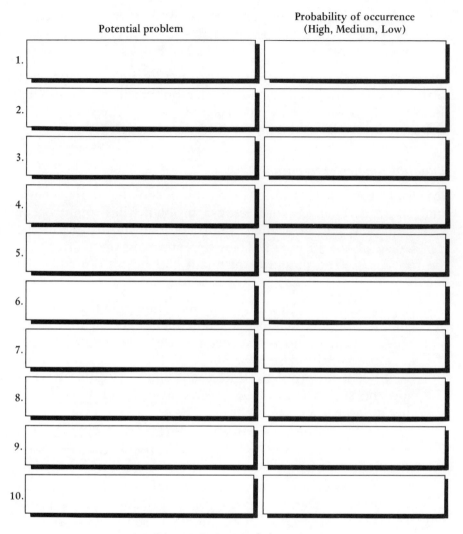

Figure 5–3. Worksheet A

by substantial analysis and "preventive thinking." As you proceed with your plan remember to:

- Communicate the intent of your plan clearly
- Stick to your plan
- Don't panic if an unexpected situation occurs
- Have contingency actions prepared for the unexpected
- Keep the natural team totally informed and involved

Seriousness of potential problem

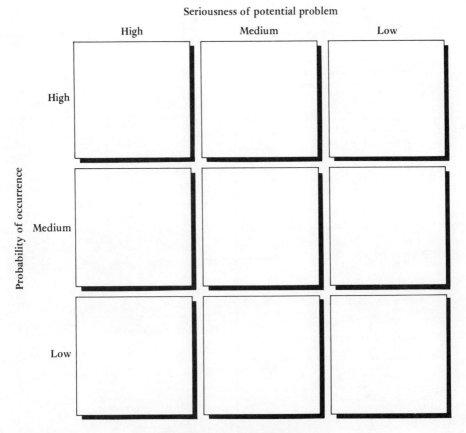

Figure 5–4. *Worksheet B*

- Listen to the process
- Don't jump to conclusions
- Document changes
- Verify results
- Update the process flow diagram to reflect implemented improvement
- Change measurements and procedures to make the "new" process people independent
- Change management measurements and practices to make the process "management proof," i.e., the measurements and management expectations must be congruent with the expectations of the team and in concert with the capability of the process.

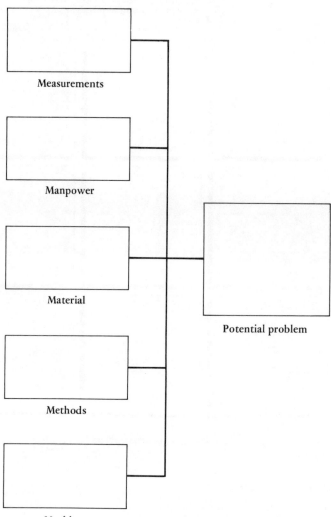

Prevention Structure Tree

Figure 5–5. *Worksheet C*

Implementation Matrix

This simple matrix (Figure 5–7) was created for you to track and record:

- The steps necessary to successfully implement your process improvement plan
- *What* action is taken

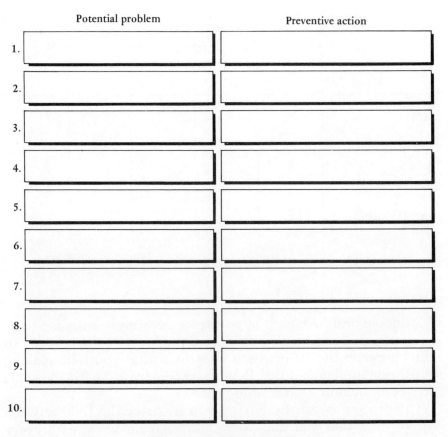

Potential problem   Preventive action

1.

2.

3.

4.

5.

6.

7.

8.

9.

10.

Figure 5–6. Worksheet D

- *Who* is responsible for the action
- *When* it occurs
- *Where* the action occurs
- *Why* it is being applied, i.e., the root cause being eliminated

Since it is a visual tool used in conjunction with the process flow diagram, it is recommended that you attach a copy of it to your PFD. Keep it up to date and on display. It is a powerful communication tool that can be used within your team and to communicate action, intent, and progress to your management team. If you look closely, you will see that a completed matrix is an indication of a completed implementation plan.

	WHAT?	WHO?	WHEN?	WHERE?	WHY?
PLAN					
ACT					
VERIFY					
INSTITUTIONALIZE					

Figure 5–7

Continuing the Process

Continuous improvement of your process simply calls for recycling of what you have learned, applied, and experienced. To quickly recap the events, it is suggested that you follow along with your implementation flow chart (Figure 1–1). All the steps are there including "Where to next?"

The process began by having you discover the link between the process that you and your natural team work with every day and the plans and goals of your business management team. Chapter 1 showed you how to understand why your process was chosen as a focal point for process improvement. It also gave your team a better understanding of the value your process has in providing products and services to your customers.

In Chapter 2, by using process flow diagraming, you were able to get started with a logical sequence of events that would ultimately lead to continuous improvement of your process and others critical to your business.

Selection of the single most critical, highest impact area to improve your process with the least effort was accomplished in Chapter 3. Through use of process flow diagraming, Pareto analysis, and the Nine Block, you were able to:

- Identify what to do first
- Create a list of opportunities for selection of future "critical" areas for improvement

Now that you have been able to address the first item on the list, it's time to reflect on that list once more and begin the process all over again. Reference to Figure 1–1 will show you the path to continue the improvement process.

One of the most important things leaders in the corporate arena must do in the 1990s is to provide a path for people to use to succeed rather than giving them a formula that has been concocted. CPI provides you with some tools, a path flexible enough to apply to any business process, and a way of getting started. It's up to you to continue the application process and help others apply it to their processes. Through experience, you and others like you have made it work. If you act as a champion and agent for change you can make the process part of your work life.

Best Practices

There will come a time when you will have exhausted the capacity of your innate team skills and expertise to significantly improve your process. That may be the time to call on some "best practices." This subsection was created to:

- Introduce the idea of a best practice
- Help you decide when to use a best practice to improve your process
- Know where to go for help in applying a best practice

WHAT IS A BEST PRACTICE?

Let's begin this discussion by first looking at Webster's definitions of each word:

Best: Of the most excellent sort, surpassing all others; most suitable, most favorable, most desirable, most profitable, etc.

Practice: To use one's knowledge of; work at, esp. as a profession.

Combining the information from Webster and taking some personal license we can formulate a working definition:

Best practice: The use of knowledge which surpasses all others to attain the most suitable, most favorable, and most profitable results

As you might expect, there is no single best practice for all businesses or business processes. Varying processes may require different practices or techniques that are narrowly focused on a specific need.

Let's turn our attention to selecting one best practice over another.

SELECTING BEST PRACTICES

There is a tendency in our society to create and use "better mouse-traps" oftentimes to the detriment of the business and in conflict with customer needs and expectations. A best practice must be carefully selected only after the determination has been made that it is actually needed.

Therefore, before selecting a best practice to improve or enhance your process, ask yourself these questions:

- Have we done all we can to improve the process with the simple conventional tools?
- Can we fulfill customer expectations using the improved process?
- Can we meet business goals with the existing, improved process?

If you cannot answer these questions to the satisfaction of your team, then the process probably "needs fixin'." It's also probably a candidate for selection and implementation of a best practice. All you need to do now is figure out which one you need.

It is not my intent to present an exhaustive menu of best practices or guidance in the selection process. That far exceeds the scope of CPI. However, to provide some assistance, a brief list will serve as a starting point.

1. Management
   - Project management
   - Leadership practices
   - Negotiation skills training
   - Financial management practices
2. Product/process Design
   - Taguchi
   - Design for simplicity

- Design to cost
- Continuous flow
3. Process management
   - Statistical process control
   - Station control

You need to develop your own menu—one that is both specific to your business and particular to your process. You may find assistance from a training organization helpful in compiling your menu. Remember to look to the members of your team for ideas and assistance. Once you have exhausted internal resources, look to outside resources such as universities and consulting organizations specializing in your area of expertise. Look also to the same resources for training.

A sample summary has been prepared to describe a well-known "best practice." Use the description and summary outline as a guide to develop and catalog your own menu.

Best Practice Summary

PRACTICE:

Taguchi

OBJECTIVES:

To determine the sensitivity of product and/or process design characteristics to determine design characteristics that minimize the variability in product or process performance

DESCRIPTION:

This technique enables you to simultaneously vary and analyze product and/or process design features to determine susceptibility to system perturbations and variations. A set of experimental tests are performed with features held at preselected conditions. Test results are normally analyzed by computer techniques which leads to optimization of design conditions by reducing the effect of minor variations.

Once you develop your personal business menu, I suggest that you create a summary sheet similar to this so that you can describe the best practices in a brief, concise manner.

No matter how good your project results or process improvement may be, unless the information can be effectively communicated, it may lie dormant and untapped. The objective of the following three sections is to help shore up your communication skills and provide you with some tools to "stack the deck" in your favor when making a presentation, documenting project results and plans, and when holding team meetings.

Making a Presentation

The objectives of this section are:

- To provide you with or enhance some basic presentation skills
- To develop roles for team members
- To help you understand the expectations of the people to whom you are presenting your information
- To emphasize the importance of "environmental" factors in making a presentation
- To help you maximize "buy-in"

The objectives will be accomplished as you are introduced to the following topics:

- Timing
- Delivery skills
- Environmental factors
- Knowing your audience
- Making a dry run
- Some things to remember

Timing

Over the years of buying and selling real estate in different parts of the country, my wife and I discovered that there are only three things you need to consider. They are:

1. Location
2. Location
3. Location

Similarly, when you are making a presentation, the three most important considerations are:

1. Timing
2. Timing
3. Timing

Having a well-prepared message is one part of the equation. Knowing what to say and how to say it is yet another. But they are all irrelevant if your timing is off. If you say too much or say it too fast your message will lose its impact. Getting things out of sequence may also frustrate you and allow your audience to take control of the situation.

Remember to develop an implementation plan and then stick to it. If you don't, chances are you will lose control and end up "spilling your candy in the lobby." You want to maintain control and dispense the candy only when you are ready and only when you can get the most benefit from it.

Remember, timing is everything!

Delivery Skills

Every person on your team has contributed value. Therefore, everyone has a role to play. It is up to every team member to recognize and reinforce each other's capabilities and talents.

However, no two team members will have the same skills. Some may have strong platform skills and therefore could handle verbal delivery of the presentation. The skills of others may be in graphic support, storyboarding, some other area. In any case, you must:

- Identify the person with the best delivery skills.
- Select an alternate or co-presenter with delivery skills that should be developed.
- Cultivate platform skills in all team members by encouraging participation. Don't overencourage. You don't want to instill fear or intimidate. Encourage involvement and recognize all

talents during the presentation—data analyst, PFD leader, statistical process control expert, etc.

Environmental Factors

The environment plays a strong role in the success or failure of a presentation. You must be prepared to use the positives to your advantage and be able to nullify or neutralize the negative factors. Some environmental factors to consider are:

- Room size
- Location
- Time of day
- Time of year
- Temperature
- Business climate
- Attendees

Piggy-back off this list and add some of your own ideas.

Knowing Your Audience

Knowing your audience is second only to timing. You must prepare the right message for the right audience. You will usually be making a presentation to your management team; therefore it would be wise to focus on some cardinal rules of presentation to management.

1. Tell them what you are going to do.
2. Never ask them how to resolve a situation. You may get help that you would rather not have.
3. If you do need help from management, present them with at least two alternatives, then ask for advice. You must be willing to accept either solution without argument.
4. Illustrate their personal benefits associated with implementation of your plan. This is how you establish "Buy-in."

All these things will help stack the deck in your favor. Remember, there must be something in your plan for most everyone in the room. It's up to you to find out "What kind of candy they like." Then be prepared to hand it out as required to get buy-in." Always be prepared to give away some of your own candy if it helps get the plan implemented for the ultimate benefit of the customer.

Making a Dry Run

Remember the preventive measures you were urged to take when implementing corrective actions? Well, the same applies here. Why? Because Mr. Murphy is in the audience waiting for you to stand up. Even though you have thought everything through several times, something can go wrong. The proven steps to minimize the pitfalls and bear traps are to:

- Prepare your presentation
- Develop flip charts or overheads
- Brainstorm environmental factors with team members
- Conduct a dry run with a relatively friendly audience

You want to come across as knowledgeable and honest, and you don't want any surprises in the actual meeting. Performing a dry run will help:

- Discover blatant discrepancies
- Avoid embarrassing situations
- Involve others in your plan
- Maximize the opportunity for success

Expand this list to add some benefits of your own.

Some Things to Remember

If you have had the opportunity to do public speaking, you probably have developed your own style. That's OK. However, some important tips are included here to assist in improving your platform techniques and to maximize the effect of your presentation.

- *Listen:* A very important part of delivering a successful presentation is active listening. If you listen closely, your audience will tell you when to stop, interact, proceed, etc. Listening will help you with your timing.
- *Paraphrase:* Listen to questions or comments and then tell in your own words what you think you heard. In some cases

you will find out you didn't hear what was really said. In others you may find you heard much more than was expressed.

- *Involve the audience:* Monologues are one-way communication. A dialogue invites and encourages people to participate.
- *Move around:* Standing in one place while presenting your material is boring. Movement shows enthusiasm and confidence.
- *Be enthusiastic:* Show your energy and personal involvement with your subject. It is contagious.
- *Use humor carefully:* Don't be afraid to inject humor. However, be careful of your timing and your audience. It can, and sometimes does, backfire!
- *Anticipate:* Be prepared for the question that will corner you. Don't try a snow job. Be prepared to say "I don't know but I'll find out."

Project Requirements

Part of effective communication is preparing your audience with enough information so that they know what to expect each time you make a presentation. Information must be thorough and concise. Here you are given a minimum requirement list to accomplish and document a successful improvement plan. The list will also assist in the formulation of a project format to be followed so you can more easily institutionalize process changes.

- *Process Flow Diagram.* The working portrait of your process is essential to success of your improvement process because it:
  - Enables your team to visualize the process rather than just the equipment, people, or products associated with it
  - Helps identify opportunities for improvement
  - Aids "buy-in" by ad hoc members
  - Facilitates training of new team members

- *Critical-to-quality elements.* These are the process elements that have the greatest impact on process improvement and the ability to meet customer expectations.
- *Pareto analysis.* This analysis helps identify what to work

on first and what to work on next. It ties the cost factor into the judgmental process.

- *Nine Block.* This is another judgmental tool that helps prioritize improvement actions and track results.
- *Root cause analysis.* This tool brings systematic logic to judgmental problem solving. It not only serves to establish the root cause of a problem but it can also be used to analyze a potential problem situation to help prevent or neutralize it before it occurs.
- *Control charts.* When control charts are attached at the measurement points in a process flow diagram they provide a means of listening to a process. With a little imagination they can be applied to almost any process. Because you can dialogue with your process through "process focused" measurements, it is important to maintain and interpret charts on a regular basis. They are *active listening devices,* not merely places to display data. Copies of charts should be filed with process information to provide a historical record of process activity. And since they are an integral part of the PFD they must be posted together to give you a total picture of your process.
- *Timeline.* The timeline lets you communicate
  - What you have done
  - What you intend to do
  - When you intend to do it

- *Summary Sheet.* A one-page summary sheet is an essential part of your project. Even if a presentation or meeting is cut short, there must still be a means of transmitting the basic information. The format that was presented in Chapter 1 may be modified to fit your needs and the expectations of your customers.

———————

Project Summary Sheet

TEAM FOCUS:

AREA OF OPPORTUNITY:

PROBLEM STATEMENT:

ACTION PLAN:

VERIFICATION OF RESULTS:

INSTITUTIONALIZATION PROCESS:

CONTINUING ACTIONS:

Team Meetings

Team meetings are held for a specific purpose and are not to be taken lightly. You are getting together to discuss or act on your part of the business. The following list gives you some idea how other teams have chosen to use team meetings:

- Review progress.
- Establish team needs to attain goals.
- Define and assign action items.
- Define new goals.
- Present plans and progress.
- Celebrate attainment of goals.
- Present continuous improvement plan to management.

The meetings must be focused and organized to be productive. Some ways to ensure this follow.

Meeting Schedule

A scheduled meeting must be treated as a sacred event. Once a meeting is set, you must:

- Schedule other business around it.
- Always attend the meeting.
- Be on time.
- Come prepared.

- Always support the team.
- Contact the team leader in advance if you can't meet your commitments so there are no surprises in the meeting.

Remember, if you fail to meet a commitment or any of the team guidelines, you are impeding the improvement process. If you are inhibiting improvement, then you are not part of the solution—it doesn't take a rocket scientist to tell you that you are part of the problem!

Reporting Format

Every team must develop its own reporting format because each process and improvement plan is unique. After you develop your format, stick with it. Some guidelines are included in the following subsection.

Format

Consider the following items when designing your meeting format:

- How long will they last?
- What is the order of business?
- Who will lead the meeting?
- How will you record activity and action items?

The needs of teams will differ depending on their process or environment. Plan your meetings to be as productive as possible.

Frequency

Team meetings should be held at least weekly. Any less frequent and you tend to lose constancy of purpose and begin to act individually, rather than as a team.

Emergency sessions may be called by any team member. Once a meeting is scheduled, it must not be canceled.

Presenting Plans and Progress

When presenting plans and progress reports, always remember that results should be announced along with plans to continue the process. For most businesses this represents a paradigm shift because almost everyone in management is conditioned to focus on the bottom line and the short-term results associated with their perception of success. Therefore, it will take a concerted effort on the part of managers and those who work for them, not only to present the expected and necessary results, but to include an open and robust dialogue on the plans to continue the improvement process. It is incumbent upon those people who own the daily work processes to offer up the plan of continuation, and it is the responsibility of the management team to seek out plans as part of the normal means of carrying on a business team dialogue.

Location

Meetings should be held in a quiet room with a door that can be closed to create privacy. There should be space to set up a permanent storyboard to record your process and team activity.

The most successful teams have chosen to invite their management team to their "War Room" for progress presentations. This works very well because it helps managers practice "management-by-walking-around."

Attendees

The name of the permanent team and the names of all team members must be posted in the meeting room. Ad hoc member names are added as required. As team members change because of job assignment, promotion, and so on, the member list must be adjusted accordingly.

Ground Rules

- Be on time.
- Come prepared.
- Be supportive.
- Be open.
- Be noncritical.
- Be creative.
- Be flexible.

- Think "prevention and improvement."
- KISS.
- Have fun.

The Role of Management

Management plays a very critical role in the CPI process because managers are the key to making change happen and become permanent. The environment created by a manager or management team can spell business success or it can toll the death knell. We want to avoid the latter and focus on ways to reinforce the former. This section is designed to help the sponsoring manager to:

- Understand his or her management style
- Explore the working environment
- Classify current role
- Determine desired role and how to attain and maintain it

Management Styles

People can be generally classified into one of three categories,

- Leaders
- Followers
- Those who get in the way

Since managers are people (some employees would contest that biological fact) they fall into one of the same three categories. I call these management styles. You've probably seen them all. If you are a manager yourself, think about your style as we proceed. You will have an opportunity to grade yourself and identify what you like and what you might want to change.

The Environment

The environment in which the team works sets the tone for team health and success or failure. This environment depends in large part on the manager. Oftentimes you hear comments about people needing to change their attitude toward their work. Attitude is a direct function of environmental factors, and if attitudes are to change, the environment must be adjusted to enable those within it to change. In plain words, without the proper environment you will most often get an improper attitude. Recalling the ground rules will give you a hint about the environment the manager must create:

- Open
- Supportive
- Noncritical
- Positive
- Sharing

If you haven't already guessed, the role of the manager in this environment must be that of a *leader*.

Characteristics of a Leader

Do not get the idea that the environment is solely the responsibility of the manager. It is the responsibility of all team members to help create and maintain the environment. To do that, each and every person must exhibit leadership characteristics. To help you better understand what this means, a brief list of leadership characteristics has been compiled for you. You are urged to add to the list.

- Supportive
- Noncritical
- Listens actively
- Provides positive feedback
- Gives feedback honestly
- Supports change
- Shares thoughts and ideas
- Supports new ideas

To expand the list, think about the characteristics or traits of a manager you consider to be a true leader.

If you are a manager, think about the following three questions and then honestly grade yourself.

1. What type of manager am I?

- Leader?
- Follower?
- One who gets in the way?

2. Which one do the members of our team think I am?
3. Which one do I strive to be?

If you are a team member other than a manager, replace the word "manager" with "team member" and answer the same questions.

Use the answers as a starting point for open discussion about your team's environment. Remember, you must be willing to stretch yourself if you wish to remain flexible. The ability to carry on a dialogue in a trusting environment is a sign of a mature, healthy team.

Recalling the management styles mentioned earlier, you can characterize effective leaders as those who are able to lead *and* follow *and* get out of the way. The trick is knowing when to do each one. The biggest barrier to steps two and three is a psychological thing called ego. To be an effective leader you must be able to put your ego in your back pocket, stand aside, and let things happen. It is tough, but very rewarding.

My Role

Whether or not you are a manager, from here on you must decide what role you will play in the success of this process. I urge you to develop a list of things you must do personally to ensure successful implementation of the methodology in your natural work area. To help you develop your list, think about what you must do in order for your team's process to provide products or services that meet or exceed the expectations and requirements of your customers.

Commitment

When it comes time to make something happen, whether you are a manager or an individual contributor, you can't wait for someone else to take the lead. If you do, you may never see your dream come true. Therefore, you must have the "fire in your belly" and the commitment to be a leader. This requires you to:

- Be action oriented.
- Take charge.
- Make something happen.

However, just because it begins with you does not mean that you can accomplish it on your own. As we have reiterated in earlier chapters, it takes focused, selfless teamwork to accomplish goals.

I would like to launch you and your team on the path to making CPI a successful and integral part of your daily life with my personal definition of *commitment:*

If it's to be, it's up to me to get a dream started.

However, to make the dream happen, commitment must take on a new meaning from a team viewpoint:

If it's to be, it's up to us!

—TO BE CONTINUED!—

Index

Add value, 107
Application, on-the-job, 77
Applied cost, 116
Assignable cause(s), 146–147

Benefits, business, 9
Best practices, 163–166
Boundary, process, 61, 62
"Black hole," 74
Brainstorming, 28–30, 33, 71, 72
Business goals, 114

Case study, 16–18, 19–26
Cause and effect, 17, 89
Charting
  analytical data, 28
  control, 29
Coach(es)
  business, 15
  on-the-job, 15
  -in-training, 36, 38
Coaching, 15
Commitment, 41–43, 177, 178
Cp, 111
Cpk, 111
Canada, 125
Capability, 130
Cause
  common, 121
  special, 120
Control, 61, 62, 120, 121
Control chart(s), 126–129, 171
  attribute, 128–129
  constructing a, 127
  construction of x, R, 137–139
  interpretation, 141, 143–145
  practical use of, 131–149
  selection, 141–142

types of, 128
variable, 128–129
Control charting, 17
Control limits, 115, 129–131, 142
  calculating new, 148–149
  calculation of, 131–135
Co-ops, vii, 14
Corrective action, implementing, 153–154
Costs
  direct, 10
  effective, 12
Critical-to-quality, 26, 73, 170
Critical characteristics, 106
Customer, 8, 11, 13, 61, 62
  expectations, 4, 73, 164
  internal and external, 32
  requirements, 73
  satisfaction, 3, 9, 85
Cycle time, 3, 107, 116, 118

DEFCON, 19, 23, 25, 81
Defect concentration diagram, 100–102
Definitions, 2, 5, 29, 36, 39, 107, 111, 115
Dice, 124

Empowering the team, 15
Enabling the team, 15

Facilitator, 32
Feedback, 121
5Ms, 89–91, 125–126, 147
Five whos, 13
Five whys, 13
Frequency chart(s), 95–100

General Electric (GE), 27, 40, 47, 124, 125,
  131, 132, 140, 142–145, 153
Ground rules, 4

"Hitchhike," 93

Iceberg effect, 9–11, 47, 75
Implementation, 157
  flow chart, 25, 27, 153
  matrix, 160
Improvement(s), 3, 5, 7
Improvement habit 8, 153
Input, 61, 121
Institutionalizing change, 25, 46, 147
Inventory queues, 73
Ishikawa, 94, 95

K.I.S.S., 5, 100, 113, 140

Leader, characteristics of, 176
Leadership, 4
Listening, active, 4
"Listening points," 75

Management
  role of, 175
  styles, 175
Management proof, 159
Management-by-walking-around, 174
Measurements, 155
Michelangelo, 31
MRB, 11, 74
Measurement(s), 74
Mechanism, 61, 62, 67
Methodology, 2–4
Mission, 13
Multivoting, 86

"Natural" work area, 76
Nesting, 64–66
Nine Block, 85–86, 157, 159, 162, 171
Nonconformities, 133
Non-value-adding, 7, 8, 24, 25, 71, 72
Normal distribution curve, 122, 123

Ohno, Dr., 11
On-the-job coaching and application, 15
Opportunities, 19
Out-of-control conditions, 142, 147, 148
Out-of-control processes, 146
Output, 61
Overhead, 116
Ownership, 7, 15, 35, 38, 93

Paraphrase, 169
Pareto, 155, 162
Pareto analysis, 17, 51, 54, 55, 79, 80–85,
  170
Penn State, viii

Piselli, Robert, 123
Potential problem prevention, 154, 157
Presentation skills, 166–170
Prevention, 6, 10
Preventive thinking, 158
Problem prevention, 152
Problem-solving, 28
Problem statement, 86–88, 102
Process, 2, 3, 7, 62–67
  business, 7, 8, 16
  capability, 105, 110, 111, 114, 115, 123
  capability indices, 111
  center, 142
  control, 123
  communicating with, 106
  manufacturing, 7, 9
  selected, 12
  streamlined, 7
Process flow diagram, 118, 130, 170
Process flow diagraming, 17, 28, 59, 60, 65,
  67–72, 76, 106, 107
Process flow diagraming symbols, 71
Process improvement, 19–26
Process performance, 105, 106
"Process-focused," 76
Program, 6
Project summary, 48–56
Pulse, 126

QFD, 156

"Re's" analysis, 21, 73–75, 77
Resistance, neutralization of, 154
Results, 23
Rework, 11
Root cause, 8
Root cause analysis, 171
Rule of Tens, 9, 75

"Sacred cows," 77
Sample size, 133
Savings, for business, 7
Scientific discipline, 112–114
SERVCO, 1–4
Sistine Chapel, 31
Specification limits, 130
Specification(s), 105, 114
  design, 115, 118
Sponsor, 16
Sponsoring manager, 36
Stack the deck, 166, 168
Statistical probability, 144–146
Statistics, 120

Storyboarding, 17, 28, 30–35, 71, 72, 90
Strategy
  business, 8
Streamlining, 107
Structure tree, 89–92, 94
Summary sheet, 171–172
Suppliers, 3, 61, 62

Taguchi, 156, 165
Team, 3, 36
  -building, 72
  focused, 9
  management, 7
  natural, 37
  natural work, 7
Team meetings, 172
  attendees, 174
  format, 173
  frequency, 173
  ground rules, 174
  reporting format, 173
  schedule, 172

Teamwork, 10, 36
  natural, 43
Techniques, 3
Timeline, 171
Tools, 3
Toyota, 11
Training, 1, 15
Trust, 15
Turn time(s), 107

Variability, 105, 118–120
Variation, 16, 121
  characteristics of natural, 122
  natural, 120, 121
  unnatural, 120, 121, 144
Visualize, 8

Walt Disney, 31
Waste, 73
WIP, 69

Yield, 16, 18